This book is a must-have text for any researcher who is engaging with the critical incident technique. It is skillfully crafted to be useful to novice and experienced researchers alike. I wish the authors had written it years ago when I first discovered the delights (and the complexities) of this most interesting research approach.

—Caroline Bradbury-Jones, PhD, Professor, School of Nursing & Midwifery, Medical School, University of Birmingham, Birmingham, United Kingdom

---

Learn how to deconstruct complex experiences and understand the turning points that shaped them. This accessibly written book is your guide to applying critical incident technique, providing a clear step-by-step framework and practical examples to support researchers, students, and academic supervisors as they uncover valuable research findings.

—Stephanie Finan, DPsych, Assistant Professor of Psychotherapy, Dublin City University, Dublin, Ireland

---

Schwartz and Holloway's fresh presentation of the constructivist critical incident technique provides researchers with the guidance they have needed while preserving the flexibility that has been a hallmark of the approach. This practical and engaging book is one I wish I had had years ago!

—Rodney Goodyear, PhD, Emeritus Professor, University of Southern California, Los Angeles, CA, and University of Redlands, Redlands, CA, United States

ESSENTIALS OF

Constructivist
Critical Incident
Technique

Essentials of Qualitative Methods Series

ESSENTIALS OF

Constructivist Critical Incident Technique

Harriet L. Schwartz
Elizabeth L. Holloway

 AMERICAN PSYCHOLOGICAL ASSOCIATION

Published by
American Psychological Association
750 First Street, NE
Washington, DC 20002
https://www.apa.org

Order Department
https://www.apa.org/pubs/books
order@apa.org

Typeset in Charter and Interstate by Circle Graphics, Inc., Reisterstown, MD

Printer: Gasch Printing, Odenton, MD
Cover Designer: Anne Kerns, Anne Likes Red, Inc., Silver Spring, MD

Library of Congress Cataloging-in-Publication Data

Names: Schwartz, Harriet L., author. | Holloway, Elizabeth, 1950- author.
Title: Essentials of constructivist critical incident technique / authored
    by Harriet L. Schwartz and Elizabeth L. Holloway.
Description: Washington, DC : American Psychological Association, [2025] |
    Series: Essentials of qualitative methods series | Includes
    bibliographical references and index.
Identifiers: LCCN 2023058245 (print) | LCCN 2023058246 (ebook) |
    ISBN 9781433840500 (paperback) | ISBN 9781433840517 (ebook)
Subjects: LCSH: Critical incident technique. | Constructivism (Psychology)
Classification: LCC BF698.9.P47 S39 2025 (print) | LCC BF698.9.P47(ebook) |
    DDC 155--dc23/eng/20240118
LC record available at https://lccn.loc.gov/2023058245
LC ebook record available at https://lccn.loc.gov/2023058246

https://doi.org/10.1037/0000408-000

Printed in the United States of America

10 9 8 7 6 5 4 3 2 1

Contents

Series Foreword

Qualitative approaches have become accepted and, indeed, embraced within the social sciences as empirical methods as scholars have realized that many of the phenomena we are interested in are complex and require deep inner reflection and equally penetrating examination. Quantitative approaches often cannot capture such phenomena well through their standard methods (e.g., self-report measures), so qualitative designs using interviews and other in-depth data gathering procedures offer exciting, nimble, and useful research opportunities.

Indeed, the number and variety of qualitative approaches that have been developed are remarkable. The question for many of us, though, has been how to decide among the various approaches. Furthermore, many prior descriptions of the various qualitative methods have not provided clear explanations, making it difficult for novice researchers to learn how to use them. Thus, those interested in learning about and pursuing qualitative research need crisp and thorough descriptions of the steps of these approaches with lots of examples so readers can grasp how to use the methods.

The purpose of this series of books, then, is to present a range of qualitative approaches that seem the most exciting and illustrative of the range of methods appropriate for social science research. We asked leading experts in qualitative methods to contribute to the series, and to our delight, they accepted our invitations. Through the books in this series, readers have the opportunity to learn qualitative research methods from those who developed the methods and/or who have been using them successfully for years.

We asked the authors to provide the context for their method, which includes providing a rationale, situating their method within the qualitative tradition, describing the philosophical and epistemological background in terms that are easily understood, and noting the key features of the method. We then asked them to present the steps of their method in detail, including selecting a research team, sampling, biases and expectations, data collection, data analyses, and variations on their method. We also asked authors to provide tips for the research process and for writing manuscripts emerging from studies using the method. Finally, we asked authors to reflect on the methodological integrity of their approach, along with the benefits and limitations of their particular method, and to provide a list of exemplar studies so readers can get good illustrations of the approach.

The books in this series can be used in several ways. Instructors of qualitative research courses could use the whole series, presenting one method at a time to expose students to the range of qualitative research methods. Alternatively, instructors could focus on just a few approaches, as depicted in specific books, supplementing the books with examples from published studies using the approaches and providing experiential exercises to help students get started using the approaches. Other researchers will just use one book as they strive to master one qualitative approach for a specific research question.

In this book, Harriet L. Schwartz and Elizabeth L. Holloway present an excellent overview of constructivist critical incident technique (CIT). Given that many researchers are interested in specific key moments in life, CIT can help them organize how participants make meanings of these significant episodes.

Schwartz and Holloway are well positioned to help us understand CIT given their extensive body of research using this approach as well as their ability to clearly describe the steps.

—*Clara E. Hill and Sarah Knox*

ESSENTIALS OF

Constructivist Critical Incident Technique

1 CONCEPTUAL FOUNDATIONS OF CRITICAL INCIDENT TECHNIQUE

These two conversations changed my life, they empowered me more than ever. From that point on, I knew I was great. I did not have to prove it, I just needed to be in a place where I could flourish. If my immediate manager did not appreciate me, fine, I will go do something else, either within that company, or with another company. I never questioned my value or my competence after that. I was not afraid to leave a company after that conversation. I had bad bosses, but a bad boss no longer defined my success.

—Participant 3 in Viscione, 2022, p. 115

Significant conversations, meaningful interactions, and moments that help or hinder, these instances shape and texture our understandings of self and other and influence progress (individually and organizationally) toward goals large and small. The *critical incident technique* (CIT) is a qualitative research methodology, applied across the social sciences and in other domains such as health care and business to deepen understanding of lived experience and to improve process and practice through the study of incidents—some memorable years later and others important in a given week and eventually

https://doi.org/10.1037/0000408-001
Essentials of Constructivist Critical Incident Technique, by H. L. Schwartz and
E. L. Holloway

forgotten. The passage that opens this chapter illustrates the value of identifying and reflecting on critical incidents. The quote, offered by a participant in a CIT study on career advancement of Black women in Fortune 1000 companies, describes a pivotal moment in one woman's professional journey (Viscione, 2022).

WHAT IS CIT?

CIT is a structured yet flexible research methodology used to study lived experience and analyze critical or meaningful incidents or events. Researchers using CIT are positioned to explore how participants psychologically organize and make meaning of significant episodes and processes. CIT researchers may take a variety of approaches as they explore meaningful moments, uncover problem points in a system, or identify incidents that help or hinder movement toward a desired outcome.

Although CIT is typically underdocumented in reviews of qualitative methods, this technique has evolved since its development in the 1940s (Flanagan, 1947) and has gained traction across a range of domains, including business, communications, counseling, customer service, education, emergency services, hospitality, information technology, leadership, library science, management, medicine, nursing, psychology, public health, social work, and sport studies. Increasingly, graduate students choose CIT as a research method: ProQuest shows a steady increase in CIT theses and dissertations from 1 in the 1960s to 142 in the 1980s and 227 in the 2010s. Graduate students have used CIT to explore topics including recovery from occupational burnout (Woolgar, 2019), courageous followership (Paxton, 2021), and factors leading to homelessness (Stinson, 2010). CIT is valuable not only for scholar–practitioners but also for those in the field seeking to engage themselves and others in self-study and process review.

CONSTRUCTIVIST CIT

CIT is used effectively in both qualitative and quantitative contexts. In this book, we focus on qualitative approaches. Primarily, this volume introduces *constructivist critical incident technique*, a variation of the original methodology (constructivism and other philosophical foundations are discussed later in this chapter and throughout the book). CIT was developed and has been implemented primarily from positivist (Gremler, 2004) and postpositivist (Butterfield et al., 2005; McDaniel et al., 2020) epistemologies. Since the

1990s, however, researchers have moved the methodology in a constructivist direction as well (Chell, 1998; Chell & Pittaway, 1998). Because CIT itself has been largely absent in the qualitative methodological literature, this introductory chapter focuses primarily on CIT, providing a foundation for our later explication of the constructivist approach. We continue to reference and discuss CIT throughout this book to help those new to the method gain an understanding of CIT as a long-standing approach and basis for the constructivist variation. "CIT" as used in this volume serves as an umbrella term for the methodology as it has been developed and understood historically and in the current qualitative realm, whereas "constructivist CIT" indicates the constructivist-specific approach.

CIT IN ACTION

We continue this introduction by exploring examples of CIT studies and applications to help orient readers to the kinds of questions asked via this method. Following these examples, we review key definitions, philosophical foundations, and CIT in the qualitative landscape, and we consider whether CIT is a method or methodology.

Assessing Process

John C. Flanagan and colleagues began developing CIT at the University of Pittsburgh in the 1940s to analyze processes related to U.S. Air Force pilot training, success, and failure. Flanagan (1954) believed that aviation assessment processes were insufficient, as evaluators often described pilot failure in vague terms such as "poor judgment" and "insufficient progress" (p. 328). With CIT, Flanagan (1954) sought to provide evaluators with a "systematic effort to gather specific incidents of effective or ineffective behavior with respect to a designated activity" (p. 328). While Flanagan was the sole author of this method-launching article, he acknowledged in the publication that a number of collaborators and graduate students conducted similar studies as he developed the method, utilizing a critical incident approach to identify "the critical requirements" (pp. 5–6) in a variety of other professions including: education, bookkeeping, life insurance, sales, and dentistry.

Recognizing Flanagan's significant contribution, we begin with a contemporary example wherein CIT was used to assess a critical process: health care provided to women needing emergency obstetric care in northern Uganda (Alobo et al., 2021). CIT was one of two methods used to understand factors leading to maternal deaths and near-misses caused by process problems in

Ugandan health care facilities. The researchers identified critical cases and interviewed medical doctors and women who had near-miss experiences, and then they diagrammed the process of emergency maternal care for each case.

Alobo et al. (2021) found that shortages of medicine, blood, and supplies, along with referral system obstacles and gaps in staff coverage and skills, were barriers that delayed critical care, leading to maternal death or near-miss incidents. Prior studies regarding maternal mortality and near-misses focused on biological causes of death; Alobo et al. (2021), utilizing CIT and participant interviews, situated researchers to surface problems in health care services and recommend potentially life-saving changes to the process.

Exploring Lived Experience

Although Flanagan (1954) developed CIT to assess task performance through direct observation and interviews, others have adapted the method using retrospective self-report to explore meaning-making and lived experience (Butterfield et al., 2005; Chell, 1998, 2014; Woolsey, 1986). For example, Mathew et al. (2023) employed *enhanced critical incident technique* (ECIT) to study "what helped and hindered the career decision-making of 18 Indigenous young adults in Canada who see themselves as doing well in this regard" (p. 6). Through this study, researchers identified 13 categories of incidents, including networking, knowledge/information/certainty, and experience. They also drew significant conclusions with potential to influence theory and practice. For example, Mathew et al. (2023) proposed reframing career development to align with a collectivist approach: "There is a call to rethink career as a merely individual enterprise, with success and failures mostly resting on the shoulders of the one making the decisions, and to reframe it as a contribution of and to the community" (p. 14).

As demonstrated by Alobo et al. (2021), CIT is an effective method for scholar–practitioners seeking actionable recommendations. Practical application is again evident in the study by Mathew et al. (2023), as researchers identified several implications for career counseling practice, including "an important need for career counsellors supporting Indigenous young adults to have a grounding in Indigenous cultural safety and an attitude of cultural humility when doing cross-cultural work" (p. 15).

Self-Study

The process of identifying and reflecting on critical incidents can also provide meaningful opportunities for self-study, helping learners deepen engagement with their learning while educators potentially gain insight as well (Forsythe & Lander, 2003) and helping practitioners reflect and assess in the field (Brandenburg & McDonough, 2017). Stephen Brookfield, a scholar of adult learning, developed the Critical Incident Questionnaire (CIQ) to help learners consider moments they felt engaged or distanced in class as well as what they found helpful, confusing, and surprising (Brookfield, n.d.). He encourages educators to use this approach weekly to understand what is working well for students and where students are confused or disengaged and to share a summary with learners the following week. Brookfield noted that the CIQ helps him reflect on his teaching because it allows him to "see the classroom through students' eyes" (Brookfield, n.d.). In the literature we reviewed, Brookfield's writings do not acknowledge a connection between the CIQ and CIT; however, we see the CIQ as analogous to CIT so we include it here.

In related work, Brandenburg and McDonough (2017), who used critical incident identification and analysis to reflect critically on their practice as teacher educators, acknowledged both Brookfield and Flanagan as influences. Their study included teacher educators' self-assessment using the CIQ and critical incident journaling and analysis. Engaging in this process, Brandenburg and McDonough identified and reflected on critical moments during a period of substantial institutional change. They identified several themes that deepened their understanding of their experiences and led to intentional practice. For example, they recognized tensions between their personal values and institutional values, and this awareness helped them resolve this tension "without surrendering our personal values in deference to institutional expectations" (p. 229). We believe this use of critical incidents for self-study holds significant potential as a tool for workplace self-reflection and a learning approach to self-assessment.

WHAT IS A CRITICAL INCIDENT?

In the following sections, we trace the terms incident and critical as they were first used and have been developed in CIT. In addition, we provide contemporary definitions and explore alternative language and related critique.

Incident

Definition of the term incident in the CIT context has evolved over time. Flanagan (1954) classified an incident as "any observable human activity that is sufficiently complete in itself to permit inferences and predictions to be made about the person performing the act" (p. 327). As noted, Flanagan launched the method with instances collected through observation and interview. Building on Flanagan's work, other researchers began using retrospective self-reported incidents as the primary source of data, and this approach continues in contemporary CIT (Butterfield et al., 2005; Gremler, 2004; McDaniel et al., 2013; Norman et al., 1992).

Thus, we suggest the following definition: an *incident* is an event, happening, or behavior in a process or person's life that holds meaning and is recordable through retrospective recall or observation. Incidents have typically been identifiable as including an antecedent, the incident itself, and an outcome (Butterfield et al., 2005). However, incidents may not be clearly bounded with distinct antecedents and outcomes, but instead "may arise from respondents summarizing their overall experience within their description of one incident" (Norman et al., 1992, p. 590). Seeking to understand these variations in reporting, Chell (2014) proposed using the term *significant occurrences* to encompass "events, incidents, processes or issues" (p. 108) and Norman et al. (1992) suggested *critical happenings*. We discuss additional alternatives in Chapter 3.

Critical

Flanagan (1954) suggested that for an incident to be critical, it "must occur in a situation where the purpose or intent of the act seems fairly clear to the observer and where its consequences are sufficiently definite to leave little doubt concerning its effects" (p. 327). Since Flanagan, understanding of the term *critical* has typically been centered in the meaning the participant makes, rather than that of an observer. Retrospective self-report inherently relies on participants' meaning-making. Constructivist CIT researchers believe that self-reported incidents are intrinsically critical, as it is the participant's meaning-making that holds significance. Conversely, researchers with a postpositivist orientation are likely to engage independent reviewers who assess incidents "to ensure that researchers are identifying information of critical importance to the participants reliably" (McDaniel et al., 2020, p. 747). We address these philosophical foundations later in this chapter and discuss their implications for the constructivist approach throughout the book.

Alternative Language and Critique

Several CIT scholars have suggested modifying use of the terms critical and incident, particularly in specific settings. For example, when used by professionals such as health care workers and first responders, the term *critical incident* may suggest crisis situations rather than significant events unrelated to a crisis (Bradbury-Jones & Tranter, 2008; Norman et al., 1992). The term incident may be used to describe events such as patient falls and student altercations in settings such as health care facilities and schools, respectively. Thus, CIT researchers are advised to consider context when determining language to frame a study and shape interview questions.

Finally, some CIT scholars see this variation in language as a potential problem, believing that the lack of clear and consistent language may confuse novice researchers, result in inconsistent application of the method, and even lead to compromises regarding rigor. For a thorough exploration of these critiques, we refer readers to Butterfield et al. (2005), Bradbury-Jones and Tranter (2008), McDaniel et al. (2020), and Sharoff (2008). We find the variation in language to be a strength of the method, as it honors nuance and contextual factors across sectors. To maintain trustworthiness, particularly dependability, researchers who adjust language for context should make these choices explicit when reporting the study.

PHILOSOPHICAL FOUNDATIONS

CIT evolved from positivist roots and is now used primarily in postpositivist and constructivist contexts and is well-positioned for researchers working from a critical intersectional stance. For more in-depth considerations of various ontologies and epistemologies, we refer readers to *The SAGE Handbook of Qualitative Research* (Denzin & Lincoln, 2018). However, we offer the following overview to set the context for the rest of this book.

Developing the CIT method in the 1940s and 1950s, Flanagan (1947, 1954) was clearly working in a positivist context. *Positivism* declares there is a single reality that can be known and measured by an objective researcher and that research can be value and bias free (McDaniel et al., 2020). As researchers expanded the use of the method and scholars challenged positivist ideas, CIT studies were more typically designed, completed, and assessed using a postpositivist philosophy (Butterfield et al., 2005; McDaniel et al., 2020). *Postpositivism* supposes a single reality but it acknowledges that it cannot be fully known and that although researchers cannot completely remove their influence from the study, they should strive for objectivity. Postpositivism is the unstated basis of many CIT studies and is the explicit foundation of ECIT (McDaniel et al., 2020).

In the 1990s, researchers proclaimed CIT's relevance as an interpretive approach, beginning to make the case for CIT as a constructivist methodology (Chell, 1998; Chell & Pittaway, 1998). For example, Chell and Pittaway

(1998) declared "reality is phenomenal and not concrete, that data are subjective and not objective and that knowledge is socially constructed and not positivist" (p. 25). Similarly, Ellinger shifted CIT in a constructivist direction in her doctoral dissertation, wherein she sought "to capture the beliefs or mental models of managers as they facilitated learning episodes" (Ellinger & Bostrom, 2002, p. 147).

With this volume, we seek to establish a clear and comprehensive constructivist approach to CIT—constructivist critical incident technique. *Constructivism* asserts that reality is socially constructed through meanings people make of themselves and their experiences, and that there is no singular truth (Creswell & Poth, 2018). Researchers working from a constructivist stance acknowledge that they (shaped by their experiences, values, and perspectives) are present in the study and seek to understand and acknowledge their positionality while foregrounding meanings that participants make of the studied phenomenon. Table 1.1 presents an overview of constructivist CIT's key characteristics.

Given its inductive approach and centering of participants, constructivist CIT is a powerful method for researchers working from a critical philosophical stance. Unlike ECIT (McDaniel et al., 2020) in which people outside the study are often called to assess elements of the project, including incident relevance and coding, constructivist CIT centers participants and their perspectives throughout the study. Critical constructivist CIT researchers embrace standpoint epistemology (Grimes, 2001), intersectionality (Crenshaw, 2005), and cultural humility (Tervalon & Murray-García, 1998).

Beyond these initial frames, definitions of qualitative research abound and evolve. For an in-depth exploration of historical and contemporary approaches, tensions, and claims regarding qualitative research, we refer readers to *The SAGE Handbook of Qualitative Research* (Denzin & Lincoln, 2018). In addition,

TABLE 1.1. Key Characteristics of Constructivist Critical Incident Technique

Characteristic	Constructivist CIT
Researcher stance	Constructivist
Data sources	Interviews, Critical Incident Questionnaire, journals
Positionality	Researcher positionality acknowledged and articulated
Sample	Incidents as unit of analysis
Incident description	Contextualized incidents by the participant to elicit antecedent, incident, and outcome
Data coding	Structural, emergent
Data analysis	Constant comparison, interpretive, and reflexive
Reporting	Includes scope of study and researcher reflexivity

Note. CIT = critical incident technique.

please note that constructivism differs from social constructionism: "Constructivism proposes that each individual mentally constructs the world of experience through cognitive processes, while social constructionism has a social rather than an individual focus" (Andrews, 2012, p. 1).

CIT IN THE QUALITATIVE RESEARCH LANDSCAPE

Qualitative research is naturalistic (conducted in natural settings) and interpretive (concerned with how participants understand themselves and make meaning of their experiences) (Denzin & Lincoln, 2011). CIT meets these criteria as the researcher seeks to understand situated phenomena through perspectives of social actors, both the meanings they ascribe to their situations and their understandings of self. For example, Kellogg and Lidell (2012) explored "how critical incidents shape multiracial students' understanding of race and identity at predominantly White institutions" (p. 524). In addition, CIT is used effectively to study large-scale social concerns, such as the aforementioned study of health care for pregnant women in Uganda (Alobo et al., 2021) and women's experiences of microaggressions in health care systems (Piccinelli et al., 2020). Further, CIT is useful for exploratory work as well as model and theory building (Bott & Tourish, 2016; Gremler, 2004; Woolsey, 1986).

CIT and its variations are well-situated in the qualitative realm while also remaining distinct from other qualitative methods. In data collection, CIT researchers invite participants to share critical incidents and then the details around those incidents, whereas narrative and phenomenological researchers prompt participants to share the fullness of the story. Regarding analysis, CIT researchers analyze across incidents and participants, seeking to understand critical happenings. Conversely, narrative and phenomenological researchers initially keep participants' stories intact, with the intention of understanding individual experiences; narrative researchers consider how the story is told; and phenomenologists explore the essence of the individual's lived experience (Creswell & Poth, 2018).

The focus of *grounded theory* is to study social processes and propose theory (Creswell & Poth, 2018). Like grounded theory, CIT may be used to study social processes (interactions and dynamics between and among people). Whereas grounded theory helps researchers understand an overarching social process in the studied phenomenon, CIT researchers focus on critical moments within the social process. In addition, theory development is an explicit goal of grounded theory, whereas CIT can be used descriptively or to develop theory.

As noted, focus on incidents (through both data collection and analysis) rather than larger stories is the primary defining characteristic of CIT and the method's most significant difference from other qualitative approaches. This focus affords the researcher a deeper exploration of significant events that might not be considered as fully with other methods. CIT researchers prompt participants to identify critical moments in the studied phenomenon, and this invites participants to focus on and explore these key events deeply and in context (Chell, 1998; Chell & Pittaway, 1998; Ellinger & Bostrom, 2002). For example, through the CIT interview structure, the researcher prompts participants to identify antecedents and outcomes that could be overlooked in other types of interviews that invite broader storytelling.

Although CIT is clearly a substantial stand-alone methodology, researchers also use CIT in tandem with other methods. Examples include case study and phenomenology (Chell, 1998, 2014), participatory action research (Chou et al., 2016), narrative analysis (Watkins et al., 2022), and arts-based approaches (Buckner, 2012; Stephenson, 2015).

Finally, CIT is well-suited to examine issues of social change. As an inductive methodology, CIT situates the researcher to work from a critical stance (Philpot et al., 2021; Piccinelli et al., 2020), address systemic inequities (Yonas et al., 2013), and problematize extant theory and de facto practices (Bott & Tourish, 2016). CIT positions the researcher to center voices that may be marginalized or disregarded, interrogate power structures, critically examine social iniquities, and otherwise work from critical, intersectional, and decolonizing stances. CIT allows researchers to explore phenomena beyond the frames of tacitly accepted theories and to develop new theory (Woolsey, 1986). Constructivist CIT is particularly well-suited for research based on a critical or intersectional stance because it centers participants' meaning, whereas postpositivist CIT studies may not be a good fit for critical work if, for example, outside reviewers select from incidents reported, thus potentially overriding participant perspectives.

METHOD OR METHODOLOGY

Is CIT a method or a methodology? The answer to this question is complicated by the range of views regarding what constitutes method and methodology and, we suggest, by the way these terms are often used interchangeably in the literature and in research teaching and practice. For the purposes of this book, we align with the following definitions from Viergever (2019): the *methods* of a study are the "technical rules and procedures for data collection and analysis" (p. 1066), whereas *methodology* "provides guidance throughout a research study, offering one approach that links the goal of the study to the unit of analysis, to the methods of data collection and analysis and to the reporting format" (p. 1067). CIT is positioned variously throughout the literature. For example, Butterfield et al. (2005) regarded CIT as a method, Viergever (2019) considered it a methodology, and Bradbury-Jones and Tranter (2008) declared that CIT is neither a method nor a methodology, acknowledging that they had no further recommendation about how to situate CIT in this debate.

We resonate with Viergever (2019) and consider contemporary CIT a methodology. At the same time, we recognize the uncertainty that the debate between method and methodology can create for novice researchers, and we hope to allay confusion. We suggest that students will strengthen their ability and confidence as emerging scholars by seeking to understand this debate and related definitional differences, while keeping in mind that the terms method and methodology are often used interchangeably in teaching and scholarly writing.

AUTHORS' NOTE

Throughout this book, we share numerous examples of CIT studies to illustrate the range of the methodology's application and to illuminate study design and implementation. In addition, we continue to draw on the work of Pamela Viscione, PhD, who we cited at the beginning of this chapter. Dr. Viscione's 2022 study provides a powerful example of constructivist CIT. In addition, we know this study well, as we both worked with Dr. Viscione while she was a student: Elizabeth initially mentored Dr. Viscione in CIT and then Harriet served as the methodologist on Dr. Viscione's dissertation. Further, Dr. Viscione researched and wrote her dissertation while we were writing this book, so we were aware of many of her decision points and other nuances of her study.

Dr. Viscione employed constructivist CIT to identify critical incidents that helped and hindered Black women's career advancement in Fortune 1000 corporations. Her study illuminates the strengths of constructivist CIT to consider a social phenomenon from the perspective of those who live the experience. We extend deep gratitude to Dr. Viscione for sharing her work to help others learn the method and for providing feedback on an early draft of this manuscript.

Dr. Viscione's study demonstrates the depth that constructivist CIT can bring to a critical exploration of lived experience. In constructivist CIT research, the participants, their recall, and their perspectives center the study. Dr. Viscione, who previously identified as a quantitative researcher, began exploring qualitative methods and considered using grounded theory. After talking with faculty, she clarified that she was committed to understanding the phenomenon from the perspective of women who have lived it, she was interested in critical moments or turning points, and she wanted participants to declare what they found meaningful rather than having outside reviewers assess the criticality of their experiences. With this clarity, Dr. Viscione found a methodological fit with constructivist CIT.

2 ESTABLISHING METHODOLOGICAL INTEGRITY

Seeking to design, engage in, and share credible and high-quality research, constructivist critical incident technique (CIT) researchers strive to establish trustworthiness, the original and enduring standard for qualitative research (Lincoln & Guba, 2013). Despite a 30-plus-year history of qualitative trustworthiness criteria, positivist and postpositivist beliefs regarding what constitutes a quality study continue to dominate many scholarly and popular spaces where objectivity, validity, and generalizability (standards for quantitative work) are default expectations even for qualitative research. Novice researchers who resonate with constructivist epistemology may find themselves reflexively concerned with objectivity because positivist and postpositivist mindsets continue to prevail. Fortunately, as demonstrated in this chapter, qualitative inquiry offers robust criteria for establishing trustworthiness, positioning qualitative studies to stand on their own merit.

https://doi.org/10.1037/0000408-002
Essentials of Constructivist Critical Incident Technique, by H. L. Schwartz and E. L. Holloway

TRUSTWORTHINESS IN THE QUALITATIVE CONTEXT

As noted in Chapter 1, qualitative researchers seek to understand and interpret the meaning participants make of themselves and their lived experiences (Denzin & Lincoln, 2011), and this intention informs the structure of qualitative studies and the standards by which they are assessed. For example, qualitative researchers seek rich data obtained by conducting in-depth interviews with a small number of participants rather than by distributing a survey to a large sample, which would not garner the detailed and nuanced material typically gained through interviewing (Morrow, 2005). Likewise, qualitative researchers seek a purposeful sample (i.e., participants who have experience with and wish to discuss the studied phenomenon) rather than a random sample. Further, qualitative researchers typically use demographic and other contextual data to situate the study and allow readers to determine transferability. Beyond providing context for the study, these kinds of data are less important than participant meaning-making (Morse, 2018). Let us illustrate this point with an example. If a participant said, "My boss yelled at me for 10 minutes," a qualitative researcher would be far more interested in the participant's experience of being yelled at for what felt like 10 minutes, rather than whether the encounter literally lasted 10 minutes.

These elements of qualitative research—focus on meaning-making, small sample sizes, the role of rich data, and demographic and temporal details—have implications for study design and methodological integrity. In addition, qualitative researchers engage with trustworthiness as a process throughout the entire research endeavor, rather than waiting until the project is near completion and then applying trustworthiness criteria to the findings (Morse, 2018). For these reasons, we address trustworthiness early in this book to provide readers with a methodological integrity lens through which to explore designing the study, collecting data, and undertaking later phases of the constructivist CIT research journey.

TRUSTWORTHINESS IN CONSTRUCTIVIST CIT

We find it helpful to think of trustworthiness on two levels: criteria and strategies. *Trustworthiness criteria* serve as a conceptual framework for pursuing and assessing qualitative research quality and integrity. This framework guides the researcher throughout the study and provides standards by which future readers may assess the work. In seeking to manifest trustworthiness criteria, the researcher engages in *trustworthiness strategies* during the process. These strategies are the practices the researcher uses to actualize the trustworthiness criteria. Beginning the study with a clear sense of trustworthiness criteria and operationalizing these criteria with associated strategies throughout the process (a) helps the researcher feel confident in their process and findings and (b) serves to inform readers of the standards met by the study.

Trustworthiness Criteria

Striving to advance a constructivist approach to CIT, we begin with Lincoln and Guba's (1985) trustworthiness criteria: credibility, transferability, dependability, and confirmability (Table 2.1). *Credibility* consists of robust data that intrinsically supports itself and the findings. *Transferability* is a process by which readers determine the degree to which the findings apply in their context. Researchers enable readers to assess transferability by providing a positionality statement and thick description (including a clear description of the study context)—this allows the reader to determine potential application in their setting. Transferability differs from the quantitative standard of generalizability, which is determined by the randomness, representation, and size of the sample. Researchers establish *dependability* by making their

TABLE 2.1. Constructivist Critical Incident Technique Approaches to Trustworthiness

Trustworthiness criteria	Description	Constructivist CIT strategies
Credibility	Robust data and thick description that supports findings	Constant comparison, saturation, outlier incidents
Transferability	Relevance of findings and interpretation to similar contexts	Positionality, thick transcription of study context
Dependability	Consistency in the implementation of the method and transparent documentation of the research process	Coding team, audit trail, process and communication memoing
Confirmability	Findings are shaped primarily by the participants' perceptions and meaning-making, not the researcher's preconceived theories	Positionality, sensitizing concepts, tacit assumptions made apparent through reflexive and analytical memoing, coding team

Note. Data from Lincoln and Guba (1985).

process transparent through an audit trail and memoing (discussed later in this chapter) such that readers can trace the research design and implementation and understand decisions made throughout the study. Finally, *confirmability* is evident when the researcher effectively balances their involvement and interpretations so the findings and report center the participants' meaning-making and not the researcher's previous working theories.

Strategies That Support Constructivist CIT Trustworthiness

Constructivist CIT researchers engage trustworthiness strategies to work toward and support trustworthiness criteria. These strategies include the following: exploring positionality, sensitizing concepts, and tacit assumptions as well as memoing, maintaining an audit trail, working with a coding team, engaging in constant comparison, identifying outlier incidents, and reaching saturation. The following section on positionality is particularly long; this is due to the complexity of the topic and is not meant to imply that other strategies are less important.

Positionality

As critical constructivist scholars, we work from a standpoint epistemology (Grimes, 2001) and thus believe that exploring and elucidating one's positionality is an essential first step in the trustworthiness process. Standpoint epistemology "suggests that the standard notion of objectivity is neither possible nor positive" (Grimes, 2001, p. 134). This call to explore and articulate one's positionality is further supported by the American Psychological Association (2020a) guidelines for journals, which advise authors to include a positionality statement in submitted manuscripts.

Knowledge is always contextual—the assumption that one can step outside of the context they live in emerges from the experiences of those with dominant identities who can move through the world unaware of how identities shape their experiences. By extension, this claim of potential objectivity, the ability to work outside of a standpoint, has been used by those with power to discount and dismiss indigenous and other ways of knowing that are seen conversely as having a standpoint and thus bias. For example, anthropology scholars have dismissed Zora Neale Hurston's research and challenged her legitimacy as a scholar, claiming that Hurston, who studied predominantly Black communities, could not be objective (Brooks, 2021; Marshall, 2023)—a criticism not imposed on White researchers who study communities that are predominantly White.

Believing that all researchers work from a standpoint and have an ethical obligation to explore, name, and reflexively engage their positionality throughout the research process, we propose a trilateral positionality framework including sociocultural identity, insider/outsider status, and epistemology. In the next sections, we explore these elements of positionality.

Sociocultural identity. Articulating and interrogating one's sociocultural identity is imperative in the qualitative research process. Race, ethnicity, gender, sexual orientation, social class, age, physical and neurodiversity, and religion are among the sociocultural identities that contribute to one's standpoint. Deepening (and in some cases, first developing) awareness of one's identities positions researchers to enter the study with greater mindfulness regarding their assumptions and potential gaps in awareness regarding the self, participants, organizations or communities, and broader cultural context (Jacobson & Mustafa, 2019; Milner, 2007). Further, understanding one's social locations is essential to identifying potential power dynamics that may be unseen yet present between the researcher and the relevant organization or community and potential participants (Milner, 2007).

We recommend two tools for exploring sociocultural identity and positionality: Jacobson and Mustafa's (2019) Social Identity Map and Milner's (2007) framework. The Social Identity Map offers researchers a three-tier process through which to explore their social identities and locations as well as related experiences and emotions. Milner's (2007) framework offers a range of incisive questions that guide the researcher to continue exploring self, self in relation, research in community, and self and research in system.

Social identities and their salience are fluid and may even be influenced by engagement with the study itself (Jacobson & Mustafa, 2019; Milner, 2007). Given this fluidity and because trustworthiness is a study-long process and not simply an outcome, we agree with Jacobson and Mustafa (2019) and Milner (2007) and we advise researchers to engage with these reflexive processes throughout the project.

Insider/outsider status. Acknowledging that the researcher is present in the study, qualitative methodologists have named and wrestled with perceived advantages and disadvantages regarding the researcher's insider and outsider standing with the community, organization, and other study contexts (Dwyer & Buckle, 2009; Kerstetter, 2012). Insider status (i.e., being a member of the studied community) may afford researchers with easier access to participants, quicker rapport, and insights into the nuance of described experiences. Conversely, potential participants may be less likely to engage or disclose with an insider researcher, fearing judgment or a breach of confidentiality that would make them vulnerable in their community. Finally, insider researchers need to be particularly attentive regarding their assumptions and potential to project their own perceptions and working theories (of note, all researchers need to heed these cautions).

Although early discourse regarding insider/outsider standing called on researchers to claim and name either insider or outsider status, later scholars suggest a more nuanced approach (Dwyer & Buckle, 2009; Kerstetter, 2012). Moving beyond the binary of insider/outsider, contemporary methodologists suggest that all qualitative researchers operate along a continuum of insider and outsider—this framing aligns with constructivist CIT.

To illustrate some of these tensions, we consider Viscione's experience of the insider/outsider dynamic. She recalled the following:

> I would say the participants weighed my experience as a Black woman executive heavily on the insider/outsider continuum and because their dominant experience was being the first, only, or one of a few Black executives, the dominant view was that I was an insider—one of the few that could understand their experience and someone they could trust with their stories. (P. J. Viscione, personal communication, January 10, 2023)

Viscione was clearly an insider in her study and, at the same time, she had not worked in all sectors and functions represented by participants. This example illustrates that even with significant insider status, this element of positionality is most accurately understood on a continuum. Additionally, Viscione recognized implied meanings and could contextualize data in ways that might have been missed by a White researcher. Aware of her insider status, Viscione engaged in deep and devoted journaling and consultation practices to identify moments when she might have been projecting her experience such that it would overlay what she was hearing from participants.

Ontology and epistemology. Researchers also frame their study and support methodological choices by clarifying and stating their *ontology* (beliefs regarding the nature of reality and knowledge) and *epistemology* (assumptions regarding how we acquire knowledge or how we know our social worlds; Esposito & Evans-Winters, 2022; Holmes, 2020). For example, a constructivist epistemology guides choices such as interviewing until saturation and emergent coding (concepts in Chapters 3 and 5 respectively). Explicitly sharing one's ontology and epistemology also helps readers understand methodological and trustworthiness choices. For instance, a reader may wonder why the researcher did not employ a strict interview protocol but instead used a more flexible interview guide. Knowing that the researcher is working from a constructivist position allows the reader to see the interpretivist nature of the study design (this is discussed further in Chapter 3).

Positionality statement and process. Developing and remaining engaged with one's positionality statement and awareness takes time and focus, and this part of the research process is integral for conducting ethical research and offering trustworthy findings (Holmes, 2020; Jacobson & Mustafa, 2019; Milner, 2007). Engaging one's positionality is essential throughout the research process, from initial exploration, articulation, and interrogation through data collection (e.g., How is my positionality influencing who joins the study?), data analysis (e.g., How can I balance acknowledging my presence in the study and not letting my perspective override that of participants?), and study reporting. We encourage researchers to engage in reflection and process their reflective work with a trusted thought partner, colleague, or mentor before beginning the study and throughout the endeavor.

Identifying Sensitizing Concepts and Tacit Assumptions
Researchers also engage with a thought partner while developing the study to identify and interrogate relevant sensitizing concepts and tacit assumptions. *Sensitizing concepts* are theories a researcher holds when beginning the project. These theories guide the researcher's practice and influence the design and implementation of the study. For example, relational cultural theory (a human development theory) is a sensitizing concept that guided our study on meaningful interactions between students and faculty (Schwartz & Holloway, 2014). In contrast, *tacit assumptions* are more generalized than sensitizing concepts and do not stem from theory but rather from one's lived experience. These assumptions are part of everyday sense-making. For instance, the belief that relationships are important in teaching and learning is an implicit assumption we bring to our work.

A good thought partner helps us name and interrogate sensitizing concepts and tacit assumptions before we begin the study, so we are more aware of our own assumptive meaning-making. Ideally, when we have identified and interrogated our sensitizing concepts and tacit assumptions, these frameworks and beliefs remain front of mind throughout the study. This awareness helps us catch ourselves if we drift toward projecting or superimposing our own thinking such that it overrides that offered by participants. These efforts contribute to confirmability, helping us balance our presence in the study.

From a constructivist perspective, sensitizing concepts are "points of departure for developing, rather than limiting, our ideas" (Charmaz, 2014).

That is, we do not seek to prove or disprove sensitizing concepts. Nor do these concepts establish boundaries for the study. Rather, we recognize that we cannot design a study without drawing on prior knowledge, so we make that prior knowledge overt (e.g., reviewing these theories in the literature review). This transparency helps readers consider transferability by understanding frameworks brought to the research.

Memoing

Memoing serves many purposes in the qualitative research process and supports trustworthiness. For example, researchers record process memos to trace their thinking at decision points throughout the study, and this act of transparency supports dependability because it makes the researcher's process explicit. Similarly, researchers engage in *reflexive memoing* to reflect on their growth throughout the project and their identity and related matters, such as power and positionality in relation to the research process. As such, reflexive memos support dependability (as an act of transparency) and confirmability (as evidence of the researcher's work to remain cognizant of their presence in the study while also centering the participants and their stated perspectives). Through these and other types of memoing (discussed in Chapter 4), the researcher actively engages with the trustworthiness process. These memos later serve as part of the audit trail, and excerpts may even be shared in the study report to help readers assess dependability and confirmability.

Maintaining an Audit Trail

The *audit trail* is the whole of electronic and physical documentation and data, and it thus provides an overview of the study design, including essential documents such as the institutional review board (IRB) application (an IRB is a faculty committee charged with reviewing all research proposals for ethical considerations, particularly in terms of protecting the rights and welfare of human participants), calls for participants, and consent forms, coded transcripts, and memos. The audit trail allows others to follow the study from start to finish and clarify the study's methodological integrity, transparency regarding methodological decisions, and relevance in their own context.

Engaging With a Coding Team

We advise constructivist CIT researchers to engage with a coding team throughout the coding process. Keeping in mind that constructivist CIT is an interpretive process that honors standpoint epistemology and a firm constructivist stance (i.e., there is no single or objective truth), the role of the team is not to check or verify the researcher's work. Rather, the researcher and the coding team engage in a dialogic process intended to help the researcher refine and expand their interpretation of the data first through the coding process and continuing through data analysis. Engaging with a coding team also potentially helps researchers notice and course correct if their own perceptions begin to dominate their coding and other interpretive work. Consequently, these processes support credibility, dependability, and confirmability. Work with coding teams is discussed in Chapter 5.

Constant Comparison

Originating from grounded theory (Charmaz, 2014), *constant comparison* involves frequent movement among codes, transcripts, themes, and memos. This movement (e.g., returning to coded excerpts when one has identified a theme) serves to help the researcher clarify that their interpretation aligns with participants' stated perceptions and experience and to adjust if they realize they have let their views override the participants' views, supporting credibility and confirmability. This process is described in Chapter 5.

Outlier Incidents and Reporting

In some studies, researchers notice incidents that are fundamentally different from other reported incidents. Analyzing and reporting these outlier incidents helps establish credibility and deepens the analysis and report (Morse, 2015). Outlier incidents may stem from outside the dominant perspective, so reporting these incidents may include perspectives that are typically ignored and thus support credibility. Likewise, including outlier incidents can help the researcher avoid forcing incidents into existing incident types, adding credibility and confirmability.

Saturation

Saturation is achieved when themes are well-developed, robust, and supported by the data (Charmaz, 2014; Morse, 2015). Through coding and memoing, the researcher begins to see connections among categories and to develop larger concepts or themes. The researcher then works to expand and deepen their understanding of these themes by returning to earlier transcripts and codes to identify relevant data they may have missed and carrying this awareness into future interviews. To the nonconstructivist, saturation may seem like simply looking to confirm one's hunches. However, saturation is not a given; the researcher may think they see a salient theme, only to find that it is not supported in the data. Thus, when the researcher confirms "many similar instances of the phenomenon . . . certainty is incrementally built" (Morse, 2018, p. 809). Saturation supports researcher confidence in the findings, and a documented saturation process helps establish trustworthiness.

We offer this chapter on trustworthiness early in this volume so it may serve as a reference point as you progress. In the next chapter, we explore constructivist CIT study design.

3 DESIGNING THE STUDY

Constructivist critical incident technique (CIT) follows the five primary steps of CIT research design. These steps are as follows:

1. framing the study, including the context, purpose, and objectives;
2. designing the method of the study;
3. collecting data;
4. coding and analyzing the data; and
5. interpreting and reporting the findings. (Flanagan, 1954)

We begin this journey by determining the purpose of the study, crafting the research question, and framing the purposeful sample. Figure 3.1 provides a visual model of the constructivist CIT research process. We encourage you to refer to this model as you progress through this book to help you remain oriented to the various steps and processes of constructivist CIT.

https://doi.org/10.1037/0000408-003
Essentials of Constructivist Critical Incident Technique, by H. L. Schwartz and E. L. Holloway

FIGURE 3.1. Constructivist Critical Incident Technique Research Process

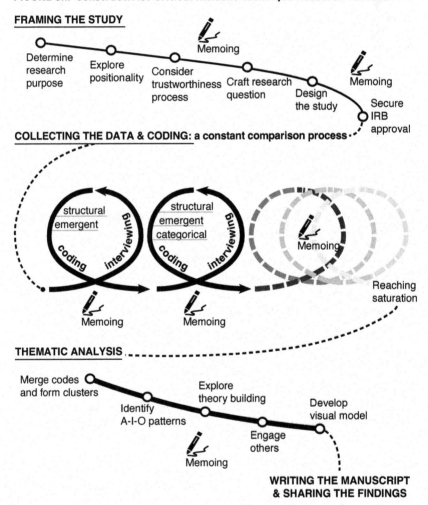

Note. A-I-O = antecedent, incident, and outcome; IRB = institutional review board.

DETERMINING THE PURPOSE OF THE STUDY

Researchers often pursue topics that emerge from their practice experiences. For example, they may notice an event that challenges previous knowledge or practices. Although CIT historically sought to explore practice, researchers also use CIT to explore established theories or generate new theory (Bott & Tourish, 2016; Fuglsang, 2017).

To begin, consider your research interest. What provoked your curiosity? Was it an experience that puzzled you and for which you had no ready explanation or a theory you wished to understand more deeply? If you remain curious and seek answers, you have begun *problematizing* the event. Problematizing does not mean the topic or experience is a problem; rather, previous approaches and strategies do not seem useful in understanding or responding to the situation. Schatzman (1991) describes problematizing as "the interrogative and analytic processes in the face of cognitive problems with phenomena, that is when recognition and recall fail to provide situationally sufficient understanding" (p. 309). Schatzman adds that the experience of troubled cognition "introduces the quest for a more analytic inquiry into the situation" (p. 303).

Scholar-practitioners interrogate situated phenomena to discover relevant and meaningful knowledge about people's experiences and meaning-making. As such, we must mention an important caveat about choosing a study topic: We have occasionally worked with students considering a research topic that was not only meaningful but also connected to their own intense or traumatic experiences. We strongly encourage students to avoid topics that may touch on their own trauma. The deep engagement required for a research project when connected to one's emotional history can be triggering. In these situations, the balance of being present in the study while not letting one's own experience and perspective overshadow that of participants can be even more difficult. The rare exception to this caution would be if the researcher were confident they had processed the trauma such that minimal unresolved emotional material remained.

Returning to your inquiry, as you reflect on your interest you begin to explore whether this question warrants further investigation. At this stage, engage thoughtfully with relevant scholarly and practice literature to consider the following questions: Will this study add to existing knowledge in the field of practice? Will this study contribute to the scholarly conversation and perhaps result in developing or expanding theory? Who are the relevant audiences, and will this study contribute to their understanding and engagement? As you reflect on practice and explore pertinent literature, you begin to frame the relevance of the research topic and the overall purpose or aim of the study.

For example, Viscione (2022) was interested in the persistent lack of Black women in corporate executive positions, a role she had occupied for many years. Although she knew from experience there were many challenges for Black women in high-level leadership roles, Viscione also knew that she and others had succeeded in reaching executive positions. Her literature search revealed a substantial body of work on the barriers Black women face in corporate America. Yet few studies sought the perspective of women who had overcome challenges and attained executive status in these settings. Viscione was interested in these women's journeys and, as mentioned previously, initially considered using a grounded theory approach. After Viscione engaged in practice interviews, she realized that she was compelled to understand key moments in these women's careers and so, in consultation with faculty, chose constructivist CIT as her methodology.

Viscione's (2022) process illustrates the layers in determining the purpose of the study: identifying and problematizing the topic, narrowing the focus, and beginning to clarify how one is driven to explore the phenomenon (e.g., the arc of stories, social processes, or, in the case of constructivist CIT, via critical incidents). Through this process, the researcher begins to assess the fit of the intended methodology with the study purpose. For example, when Viscione determined she was interested in critical moments rather than larger stories, she realized constructivist CIT was the methodology that fit her emerging question.

CRAFTING THE RESEARCH QUESTION

Once you have determined the purpose of the study and reviewed relevant literature, you are ready to begin the iterative process of crafting the research question. In our experience, novice and experienced researchers alike often craft the research question dialogically in consultation with a trusted colleague or faculty advisor, seeking to sharpen the framing of the question and refine the language. Of note, the *research question* is the question that shapes and guides the study, and it is different from the interview questions used to gather data. Box 3.1 presents sample CIT research questions.

Crafting the research question (represented in the summary statement in Box 3.2) was iterative as Viscione (2022) moved through several steps, including ongoing interaction with faculty, reflecting, and writing. In Box 3.2, the process of crafting a question is represented in each of the statements;

BOX 3.1
SAMPLE RESEARCH QUESTIONS

- What are the critical moments that generate a feeling of inclusion for professional staff in higher education institutions? (Lampley, 2023, p. 3)

- Why do men drop out of individual counseling/psychotherapy and what factors would have encouraged them to remain? (Springer & Bedi, 2021, p. 776)

- How do critical incidents shape multiracial students' understanding of race and identity at predominantly white institutions? (Kellogg & Liddell, 2012, p. 524)

BOX 3.2
FRAMING THE RESEARCH QUESTION

The problem at the core of this study is the underrepresentation of Black women in executive-level positions at large, primarily White corporate organizations. The overall question is why the underrepresentation persists. The more targeted overall question for this study was what are the most impactful events that help or hinder the advancement of Black women to executive-level positions in predominantly White large companies in the United States? (Viscione, 2022, p. 18)

Viscione moves from the topic (underrepresentation of Black women) to focused problematization (why underrepresentation persists) and then to the research question (What are the most impactful events?).

CLARIFYING INCIDENTS AND CONTEXT

At this stage, the researcher further clarifies and designs in accordance with their research objectives, focusing on incident types and the study's context. Let us return to Viscione's (2022) process: Once she felt clear she would use constructivist CIT and explore incidents, Viscione then considered whether she would take an open-ended or binary approach, meaning whether she would ask for four incidents (without framing incident types) or categorize the types of incidents sought (e.g., two positive and two negative or two that helped and two that hindered). Although she was interested in hearing about incidents that helped and hindered, Viscione decided not to indicate incident types when engaging with participants, as she wanted them to share whatever incidents they deemed critical. At this stage of the process, the researcher, often in consultation with faculty or a research partner, further clarifies the study context. In Viscione's case, she chose to focus on Fortune 1000 companies.

RECENT OR DISTAL: DESIGNING FOR RECENCY AND RECALL

The constructivist CIT researcher must decide whether to seek recent events, establish a longer time frame (e.g., ask for incidents from the last 5 years), or enter the study open regarding the timing of occurrences. Typically, the research question dictates the approach. For example, in Chell's (1998) case study of a micro business that experienced a dramatic set of events, she asked interviewees to reflect on the development of the business over the previous 5 years and circumstances with positive or negative impact. Conversely, in our study on meaningful interactions between students and professors, we sought to explore incidents that were important in a given week but may or may not be significant years later (Schwartz & Holloway, 2014). Thus, we contacted student participants weekly to ask if they had experienced meaningful interactions with faculty, and we scheduled interviews as needed. In contrast, Viscione (2022) was working with an open timeframe and she was able to collect up to four incidents per interview, so she only needed to meet with each participant once (note that time commitment is an important consideration, particularly for graduate students working to complete their studies). These choices may seem obvious but require intention when framing the study and developing the interview guide.

Recency of Events

Constructivist CIT studies seek to identify events of significance in an individual's life experience. Thus, the research design should account for the differing nature in which events are remembered (Edvardsson & Roos, 2001). The recency of an event, emotional arousal during the event, and the positive or negative nature of the event all influence recall (Petrucci & Palombo, 2021). In general, if participants are asked to reflect over a specific time frame, they will report a greater number of recent rather than distal events because they will have more uncertainty around the details of distal events (Bradburn et al., 1994). However, Petrucci and Palombo (2021) found that events involving emotional arousal (i.e., the types of events often requested in critical incidents) are recalled more readily than recent events with less emotional content. Details of distal events and their sequencing may be enhanced "if the items are compositive pieces of a broader emotional plot, as attention would be allocated to their connections" (Petrucci & Palombo, 2021, p. 1505). Thus, the contextualization of critical events through storytelling, as reflected in constructivist CIT and other phenomenological (Chell, 2014) and narrative (Watkins et al., 2022) approaches to CIT encourages detailed recall in reporting. Additionally, scholars of autobiographical memory posit that the centrality of an experience to one's identity influences recall of emotional experiences across time, regardless of whether the event is positive or negative (Pociunaite et al., 2022, p. 624).

From the vast literature on memory and recall of autobiographical events (i.e., events of interest in constructivist CIT), we draw on two primary principles from Petrucci and Palombo (2021) to consider in the research design. First, positive and negative events are more readily recalled than neutral events regardless of recency. Second, the sequence or temporal order of events and details of the context, duration, and personal emotional reaction are enhanced when part of a larger story (Petrucci & Palombo, 2021).

Adapting Data Collection Strategies to Address Recall

For examples of how researchers might adapt their data collection plan to address the complexities of recall, we turn to studies in nursing (Keatinge, 2002) and communication (Kamal et al., 2021). The day-to-day routine of ongoing nursing care necessitates data collection approaches that consider the potential limitations of recall so the researcher can explore seemingly ordinary practice actions that might result in challenging and significant situations of research interest (Norman et al., 1992). Keatinge (2002) was interested in studying the neonatal nurse practitioner role. To gather relevant incidents, a nurse/researcher from another specialty observed two nurses, recorded "significant" incidents that occurred in everyday practice, and noted a description of the context or situation, the action taken, the significance of such an action within the context, and the outcome or potential outcome. These observations were helpful in triggering the recall of potentially critical events during the day's activities. The nurses were then asked to reflect on the events.

In a different data collection adaptation, Kamal et al. (2021) used social media to prompt recall. In a study of familial communication bonding patterns, the researchers introduced a modified CIT approach to mitigate incomplete participant recall of mundane interactions. Kamal et al. used family members' social media exchanges to stimulate participant recall of familial exchanges and elicited participant reactions to exchanges deemed critical to bonding. The authors argued that uncritical [*sic*] incidents in messaging should also be included in the data collection to provide a broader picture of messages both critical and uncritical that are enacted in familial communication patterns, thus allowing participants to choose those exchanges they considered most meaningful.

THE PURPOSEFUL SAMPLE IN CIT

CIT researchers use *purposeful sampling* (also called purposive sampling), as is typical in other qualitative methodologies. Whereas quantitative researchers are more likely to invite large random samples, qualitative researchers seek small samples of people who have experienced the studied phenomenon and are interested in reflecting on and sharing the meaning of their experience (Creswell & Poth, 2018). In addition, constructivist CIT researchers intentionally strive for an inclusive sample (Esposito & Evans-Winters, 2022). Thus, we advise researchers to consider how their identities may influence who responds to calls for participants and how their presence may influence participant self-disclosure in the interview (for further discussion of identity and power dynamics in the study, see Chapter 2, this volume).

Participant Criteria

With purposeful sampling as a guide, the researcher determines the participant criteria. These criteria typically include demographic elements, such as participants' cultural, social, or professional identity and roles and their lived experience in a specific community context or with a specific event. For example, Viscione's (2022) criteria were as follows:

> The participant criteria for this study were Black women who achieved executive roles in Fortune 1000 corporations, with 15 or more years of management work experience in the United States. Any potential participant that had an active relationship with the researcher in the past 15 years was rejected. (p. 20)

The criteria guide researchers in writing a clear call for participants and help researchers determine whether potential participants fit the intention of the study. Now that we have considered how to frame the sample, we explore the question of sample size in constructivist CIT research.

Sample Size

Flanagan (1954) determined that the sample size in CIT should be based on the number of incidents rather than the number of participants. For example, if 5 participants each recalled 4 critical incidents, then the sample size would be 20, based on the number of incidents collected overall compared with the more traditional approach to determining a sample by counting the number of participants. This practice has endured, and incidents continue to serve as the unit of analysis in CIT studies. We advise students to seek four incidents per participant and to anticipate that most participants will likely contribute three to four. In some cases (e.g., when recruiting participants is difficult), the researcher may seek more than four incidents per participant. Although participants will not typically provide the same number of incidents, the relative balance of incidents across participants is important so one person's perspective does not dominate the study.

Working from a positivist perspective, Flanagan (1954) recommended a sample range of 50 to 100 incidents. Over time, as researchers have developed variations on the overall method and depending on epistemological stance and data collection approaches, CIT studies have included a range of numbers of participants and incidents (Bradbury-Jones & Tranter, 2008). Researchers using a CIT questionnaire often have a greater number of participants and incidents. For example, Kemppainen et al. (1998) had a sample of 273 critical incidents from 118 participants. Conversely, studies using interviews in an interpretive approach tend to engage fewer participants and have fewer incidents.

Constructivist CIT researchers determine sample size by the principle of saturation, a standard approach to concluding data collection in qualitative studies. As Bott and Tourish (2016) noted, *saturation* "occurs when additional interviews or coding no longer provide new behaviors or new codes" (p. 286) related to the study topic. Determination of sample size by saturation requires the use of a *constant comparison approach* to data collection and analysis. As noted in Chapter 2, constant comparison means moving back and forth between data collection and analysis. In practice, you may conduct one or two interviews and pause the data collection process while coding and beginning to analyze the data. This rhythm continues throughout data collection, helping to determine at any given point whether the data are saturated; that is, salient emergent themes are developed and supported by the data and no new significant categories are emerging.

Although saturation is a typical standard for concluding data collection in qualitative work, the approach is not universally accepted or applicable. For example, Braun and Clarke (2021) contested the use of saturation, particularly in reflexive thematic analysis, pointing to several issues, including the term's lack of clear definition and philosophical misalignment. We refer readers curious about the larger debate to Braun and Clarke (2021).

While saturation is typically an appropriate guide for constructivist CIT data collection, we recognize that researchers conducting exploratory studies (studies of under-researched phenomena) and those who are working with vulnerable or hard-to-reach populations may not be able to engage enough participants to reach saturation. In order for research to be possible in sensitive and unexplored domains, we encourage an alternative structure in which the researcher collects data until they have rich and detailed thematic material and relevant implications to contribute to the scholarly discourse and practice literature without reaching what would be considered saturation. The decision to forego saturation is not taken lightly but may be the only option when a researcher is working in a nascent or vulnerable space.

Although constructivist CIT researchers often determine sample size by saturation, we know that people using the method for the first time often ask for guidance regarding the number of participants they will likely seek. We have found that our students seeking binary incidents (e.g., positive and negative) often reach saturation between 70 and 80 incidents (typically gathered as 2 to 4 incidents per participant), whereas those taking an open-ended approach may reach saturation between 50 and 70 incidents. To increase confidence in the decision, we also advise conducting one or a few more interviews after you believe saturation has been reached. Viscione (2022) believed she had reached saturation at 64 incidents and then continued until she had 80. At this point, she felt confident that no new categories were emerging and the existing categories were robust and supported. Of note, saturation can be a difficult concept to grasp: It sounds easy in the abstract, but novice researchers are often less confident applying it in practice. In our experience, novice and experienced researchers alike consult with others (e.g., research partners or dissertation chairs and methodologists) to discuss and determine saturation.

CRAFTING THE INTERVIEW GUIDE

Before the constructivist CIT researcher crafts interview questions, they must resolve three elements that frame the study: (a) the language used to name an incident, (b) the incident prompt, and (c) the approach to request antecedents and outcomes of an incident.

Choosing the Term for *Incident*

As noted in Chapter 1, we advise constructivist CIT researchers to determine whether the term critical incident is appropriate to their context. In some domains, this term holds a particular meaning. For example, in health care, a critical incident may constitute a consequential or fatal error. In other situations, this term may not have a specific connotation but it may not fit the spirit of the project. In our study with graduate students, we asked participants to identify meaningful interactions (rather than critical incidents), as we believed this language would communicate our focus more clearly (Schwartz & Holloway, 2014). Researchers have also suggested terms such as *significant events* (Schluter et al., 2008), *revelatory events* (Norman et al., 1992), *dilemmas* (Hensing et al., 2007), and *happenings* or *situations* (Persson & Mårtensson, 2006) to evoke critical incidents as understood in the methodology.

Refining the Incident Prompt

Next, the researcher determines whether to further clarify the nature of the incidents sought in the study. This decision is driven by the essence of the study's purpose. For example, are you trying to identify events that share a particular quality? As noted, some researchers use a binary framework in which they seek positive and negative or helpful and hindering incidents.

In another example of refining incident character, Woolsey's (1986) study of long-term friendships initially sought experiences that contributed positively to the relationship. After piloting different phrases, Woolsey concluded that the interview prompt was best stated as follows: "Please describe a particular incident or incidents when your friend did something or when something happened that significantly strengthened or deepened the bond between you" (p. 247). Notice how her use of "strengthened or deepened" directs the conversation not just to a positive event but to an event that significantly affected the relationship. She carefully crafted the question to encourage interviewees to reflect deeply on their lived experience in the relationship. In contrast, in our study exploring interactions between master's students and faculty, we asked students to identify "meaningful interactions," a prompt with less structure than Woolsey's (1986). Again, the level of specificity of the prompt is determined by the research question and the study's purpose.

Seeking Antecedents and Outcomes

CIT researchers aim to identify incidents, antecedents, and outcomes. However, the role of antecedents and outcomes in the CIT structure is contested in the larger CIT landscape. Bradbury-Jones and Tranter (2008) argued that Flanagan's (1954) definition must be honored, that an incident is a clearly described event with an identified beginning and end—they believed that this demarcation of the incident differentiates the CIT interview from other qualitative approaches.

Conversely, Norman et al. (1992) maintained that delineation of an incident is not a requirement of CIT. They instead focused on participant description of context and the incident's meaning:

> . . . incidents cannot be abstracted from the chronological temporal flow of human experience. The meanings of critical observed happenings which are located within incidents are not created anew but are the product of previously created meanings which are carried forward from previous incidents. (Norman et al., 1992, p. 599)

The emphasis on the story and the meaning it prompts for the respondent resonates with constructivist CIT and other inductive and interpretive applications of CIT (Bott & Tourish, 2016; Chell, 2014; Fuglsang, 2017; Watkins et al., 2022). For example, constructivist CIT researchers typically use a holistic approach to interviewing. Rather than asking the respondent to divide the incident by antecedents, the central event, and outcomes, the constructivist CIT researcher begins by asking the participant to reflect on an incident of significance in their experience. If the participant does not naturally describe the antecedents and outcomes as well, then the researcher can ask the following, among other follow-up questions:

- What led to this incident?
- What was the impact? (What were the outcomes?)
- How do you make sense of this situation as a whole?

This approach encourages the respondent to elaborate on the incident and its situated meaning and significance in their lifeworld. Understanding participant sense-making is the central intention of constructivist CIT.

CREATING THE CONSTRUCTIVIST CIT INTERVIEW GUIDE

Once you have considered the term you will use for an incident, the incident framing, and the approach to eliciting antecedents and outcomes, you are ready to design the interview guide. Constructivist CIT researchers use a *semistructured interview guide*, which is a list of foundational questions that help the interviewer cover essential topics. Although the interview guide provides a road map, it is not intended to be rigid or confining. Rather the researcher asks follow-up questions and even adjusts or individualizes interview guide questions as the conversation evolves. Viscione's (2022, p. 203) interview guide (repeated for each of four incidents) is presented in Box 3.3. As a constructivist CIT researcher, Viscione adjusted the language in each interview. For example, in one interview, she might have asked, "What led you to pursue this mentoring relationship?" rather than "What led to the incident?"

Viscione's (2022, p. 203) interview guide also included preinterview prompts for herself, such as reminders to turn off her cell phone, review the purpose of the study and informed consent with the participant, ask the participant to select a pseudonym, and start the recording.

Along with questions focused on incidents, constructivist CIT researchers may also ask for *wish list items*. These items may include "those people, supports, information, programs and so on, that were not present at the time of the participant's experience, but that those involved believed would have been helpful in the situation being studied" (Butterfield et al., 2009, p. 267). We see the wish list as an important contribution to the methodology. Although it was developed in the enhanced critical incident technique context, the wish list inquiry aligns with constructivist CIT because it centers participants' lived and tacit interpretations and aspirations regarding the studied phenomenon. Asking for wish list items also enacts an intersectional approach as defined by Esposito and Evans-Winters (2022): inviting wish-list items recognizes participants as experts in their own lives and privileges their perspective over the researcher's or that of people who may hold more power in a given context.

Once the draft interview guide is ready, the next step is to seek feedback from informed colleagues who can speak to the clarity, cultural sensitivity, and

BOX 3.3
INTERVIEW GUIDE EXCERPT

✓ Please describe the incident.
✓ When did it happen? Participant' level in organization? Who else was involved?
✓ Why was the incident impactful to you?
✓ What led to the incident?
✓ What was the outcome of the incident?
✓ Did the cause, impact, or feelings about the incident change with the benefit of time?

relevance of the questions—this adds to trustworthiness. After gathering and applying this feedback, novice researchers may conduct a few practice interviews to become familiar with the questions, gain experience using probes effectively, keep within the boundaries of informed consent, and stay focused on the research topic. Practice interviews also provide additional opportunity to pilot interview questions. Note that material from practice interviews cannot be used as data in the study. Researchers who are concerned about recruiting enough participants should avoid using study-eligible participants for practice interviews and instead should interview people who have relevant experience but do not fit all criteria.

COLLECTING DEMOGRAPHIC INFORMATION

In addition to the interview guide, constructivist CIT researchers prepare a demographic questionnaire. The research questions dictate the demographic and other descriptive information gathered from participants. The questionnaire typically includes items that elicit data including gender, race, ethnicity, age, and other demographic material as well as additional information about the participant and their context. For example, Viscione's (2022) study-specific questions included participants' job function, industry or sector, and number of years in management roles.

Researchers should approach collecting demographic information with sensitivity, as disclosure of some identifying material may be seen as risky for participants. Even though we as researchers seek to protect confidentiality, disclosing identities such as sexual orientation or gender may still hold risk in some contexts. Therefore, we must weigh the value of asking for this material and consider strategies for allowing participants to opt out of certain demographic questions.

Researchers can use paper or digital forms to collect these data. When choosing digital tools, select a tool with strong security features. Store all material (digital or paper) in password-protected or locked spaces.

HELPING PARTICIPANTS PREPARE FOR THE INTERVIEW

When conducting studies that ask participants to recall distal incidents (as opposed to incidents that have occurred more recently), researchers may provide a preinterview activity to help participants recall and reflect on relevant incidents. For example, before the interview, Viscione (2022) asked participants to identify four to six impactful career advancement incidents and provided several related prompts to encourage reflection. Participants did not submit their notes to Viscione, but they could choose to draw on them during interviews when they were invited to select four incidents to share. Engaging participants in prework tends to make interviews more productive, as participants are less likely to have trouble identifying relevant incidents and may provide more detailed descriptions and reflections (Bott & Tourish, 2016; Schluter et al., 2008).

Chell (1998) developed a strategy (for use in the interview) that may be helpful in studies in which the chronology of incidents is particularly important or, we add, in cases where participants seem likely to benefit from structure. In a study exploring entrepreneur experiences (Chell, 1998), for example, the interviewer gave participants a piece of paper and asked them to draw a double-arrow line across the center of the paper. The line represented the preceding 5 years. The researcher then asked participants to mark and label significant events along the line, creating a timeline. Next, the interviewer invited the participant to choose three incidents for further discussion.

PARTICIPANT TRACKING

As an additional preparatory step, we advise researchers to create a document (likely a spreadsheet) to track inquiries and pre- and post-interview communication, coding, and all other steps in the data collection and coding process. Initially, these details may seem easy to remember without a document; but at some point, you will likely be communicating with numerous potential and current participants and with your coding team and managing your own task list. You will be far more efficient and likely to cover all steps if you track your work.

RECORDING AND TRANSCRIBING

Qualitative researchers typically choose to audio record the interview if appropriate in the cultural context and permitted by the participant. Recording the interview allows the researcher to be more present, as they know they will have a verbatim account and thus will not need to take detailed notes. (As an aside, we keep a pen and paper nearby to take occasional notes when interviewing, jotting down a topic we wish to return to later in the interview.) In accordance with the informed consent, the interviewer asks whether the participant is willing to have the interview recorded and begins recording only after consent has been obtained. Relevant to this part of the process, interviewees are often receptive to being recorded, knowing this will allow them to review the transcript for accuracy and remove any segments they wish to retract from the study.

In the next chapter, we move from designing the study to collecting data.

4

COLLECTING DATA

You have framed your research question, chosen constructivist critical incident technique (CIT) as your methodology, designed the study, and received institutional review board (IRB) approval. It is time to begin data collection in earnest. In this chapter, we focus on interviewing (the predominant data collection method in constructivist CIT), additional approaches to data collection, and memoing (an essential companion to interviewing and data analysis). Refer to Figure 3.1 to follow this process. Finally, we offer guidance regarding transcript preparation.

CONDUCTING THE INTERVIEW

The researcher begins the interview by providing an overview of the research purpose and the IRB consent form and follows with a description of the interview's structure and initial question. Generally, the constructivist CIT interview is scheduled for 45 to 60 minutes. The interviewer must be conscious of honoring the agreement established in the consent form and the

https://doi.org/10.1037/0000408-004
Essentials of Constructivist Critical Incident Technique, by H. L. Schwartz and
E. L. Holloway

time allotted for the interview on the respondent's schedule. Throughout the interview, the researcher takes utmost care to prioritize the well-being of the participants who have offered their time and energy to the project. Moreover, participant well-being is significantly more important than "juicy data" (Charmaz, 2006, p. 30). Emotions are a part of the experience of critical incidents and such recollections may provoke difficult or painful memories, even when the interview topic seems positive or unlikely to stir stress. Constructivist CIT researchers strive to be conscious of their tone as they ask questions, and they seek to monitor the depth of the interview conversation as well as participant nonverbal or facial expressions that may indicate distress. If the conversation moves close to the boundary between research and counseling, the interviewer seeks to bring the exchange firmly back to the research context. This is true even if the interviewer is a counselor outside the interview setting (role clarity for counselors, coaches, and others who work in helping roles is vital in the interview context). Practitioners and researchers are to observe "boundaries of competence" (APA Ethics Code Standard 2.01; American Psychological Association, 2017) and avoid harming research participants, clients, and "others with whom they work" (APA Ethics Code Standard 3.04; American Psychological Association, 2017). In addition, after the interview, researchers should provide participants with contact information for a free and confidential counseling resource, in case the participant wishes to seek support.

Likewise, we coach researchers to be aware of emotional demands they may experience during and after interviews. Novice researchers are sometimes surprised by the depth and emotion of participant self-disclosure and may find themselves sitting with this intensity and feeling unsettled. We advise researchers to identify people who can appropriately provide support, such as trusted colleagues who will be available to engage in confidential debriefs. When the material is particularly intense, researchers may also consult with a therapist.

A comprehensive discussion of the art of conducting qualitative interviewing, developing rapport, listening deeply, framing follow-up questions, and managing difficult interview situations is beyond the scope of this book. We encourage researchers to engage with classic and current articles and books on qualitative interviewing (Gubrium et al., 2012; Josselson, 2013; Roulston, 2022; Rubin & Rubin, 2012).

Finally, taking time to memo after the interview is integral to the data collection process. Therefore, avoid scheduling back-to-back interviews and leave sufficient time to relax, regroup, reflect, and memo.

ADDITIONAL APPROACHES TO DATA COLLECTION

While interviewing remains central to most constructivist CIT studies, researchers may draw on other approaches including observation, focus groups, and participant journaling. In the following sections, we review examples of innovative hybrid approaches.

Observation

Early CIT researchers, including Flanagan (1954), collected data by observation and analyzed the data using content analysis (Gremler, 2004). Much of this early work represents a postpositivist stance in the research design, as observers rather than participants determined the value and meaning of actions; observers rated behaviors, and the validity of their judgments was determined using statistical tests of interrater reliability (Warrens, 2015). However, there are examples of using observations in combination with interviews from a more constructivist position. The study from Keatinge (2002), described in Chapter 3 (this volume), used a combination of focus groups to identify critical concerns of new neonatal nurse stakeholders, observations of neonatal nurses by an experienced pediatric nurse to capture major care scenarios, and interviews with the nurses observed to gain further clarification and reflections on their interactions. Keatinge explored stakeholder perceptions and meaning-making by including stakeholders in designing the study and inviting them to remark on researcher observations.

Multimethod Data Collection

In exploring the experiences of multiracial college students, Kellogg and Liddell (2012) employed several data collection strategies. After conducting two pilot interviews to refine the interview questions, the researchers conducted first interviews with participants and then provided each with a journal, inviting them to document incidents "related to their multiracial identity" (p. 528). After students journaled, they engaged in a second interview to discuss their journal reflections and other critical incidents related to their identity development. Students were also invited to reflect on material artifacts and to engage in focus groups. Kellogg and Liddell created this varied data collection approach to provide participants "with different ways to express themselves" (p. 528). Of note, journaling is also a logical choice when using constructivist CIT for self-study. For example, Brandenburg and McDonough (2017) maintained reflective journals while also collecting incidents through the Critical Incident Questionnaire and email correspondence in their self-study regarding their experience as teacher educators.

MEMOING

Qualitative researchers typically engage in four types of memoing: reflexive, analytic, process, and communication (Birks et al., 2008). Through *reflexive memoing*, the researcher seeks to stay in touch with their positionality and engage critically throughout the research process to interrogate how they see themselves in relation to their topic, context, participants, interview experiences, and emerging theoretical ideas. *Analytic memoing* provides the researcher an ongoing space in which to document and think through the conceptual work of the study. Through *process memoing*, the researcher records their thinking at various decision points throughout the study, adding to dependability. Likewise, *communication memoing* serves to record communication between the primary researcher and others involved in the process, including a coding team and a dissertation chair. These memos become part of the audit trail. Reflexive memoing is particularly important throughout the interview process. Constructivists recognize that the interview is a co-construction of meaning, as they are relationally and emotionally part of the unfolding and retelling of the respondent's story. As such, interviewers' awareness of their reactions to the ongoing interview process is critical to staying fully present and guarding against bias that shifts the focus of the interview from the participants' meaning-making to their own.

We have included one of Viscione's (2022) reflexive memos in Box 4.1. In this memo, she finds herself wrestling with this central constructivist tension—acknowledging that she is inherently present in the study while striving to center the participants' stories above her own. Viscione's awareness,

---

BOX 4.1
REFLEXIVE MEMO

[Reflecting on] the impact of my personal experience on what I really hear and code. It seems impossible to separate me from the data and analysis. The words they use, the facial expressions, the stories shared all bring back memories of my experience. My memories are mine, not those of the participants. It is difficult to keep them separate.

revealed in the memo, is precisely the reflexive work that positions her to strike a trustworthy balance as a constructivist researcher.

Beyond this sort of deep reflexive memoing, researchers engage in other forms of memoing after the interview. As noted previously, your field memos recorded after the interview may include your thoughts and feelings about the process, any aspects of the interviewee's story that held meaning for you, and how the interviewee's story affected your engagement in the process. Also consider any unusual occurrences (e.g., noise interruptions, nonverbal expressions, or emotional upset on the interviewee's part) that appeared to affect your relational connection with the participant.

PREPARING INTERVIEW TRANSCRIPTS

The first step in data preparation is to accurately transcribe the audio or video recording of the interview. Researchers can choose from several transcription options, including using voice-to-text applications and transcription services or transcribing the interviews themselves (which is time-intensive). Transcriptions generated by an application or human-staffed transcription service may have gaps and errors in word usage, so researchers should review the transcript with the audio after they receive the transcription. Along with making simple corrections, the researcher may be able to recall what was said in instances where the recording is inaudible. This is another reason to review transcripts soon after they are generated. In addition, the software will not identify long silences, vocal inflection, or any other paralinguistic features evident in the recording. If these speech characteristics are essential to the research aim, they should be inserted in the transcript during review. Before the development of transcription software, researchers either paid a transcription service (this remains an option, although the researcher still must review the transcript against the audio for errors) or transcribed the interviews themselves. These latter two options are far more time-consuming than using transcription software.

Transcript preparation also includes deidentifying the document—researchers have an ethical obligation to protect participant confidentiality. All identifying information, including personal and organization names, geographic location, and any other reference that might lead to identification of the interviewee, must be redacted from the transcripts. Once all identifying information has been removed, the transcript is sent to the participant to review for accuracy, add clarifying comments, or remove information that they do not want to include in the research project. This process, called *member checking*, is an element of establishing trustworthiness.

5 ANALYZING DATA

As noted in Chapter 4, collecting and analyzing data is a constant comparison process, so researchers begin coding after the first interview and continue to move among the steps of data collection, coding, and deeper analysis until they reach saturation (refer to Figure 3.1). For ease of understanding, we have organized separate chapters regarding data collection and analysis. However, as you read this chapter, keep in mind the dynamic process of constructivist critical incident technique (CIT). In this chapter, we discuss preparing for analytical work, coding, and thematic analysis.

PREPARING FOR ANALYTICAL WORK

Prior to engaging in coding and analysis, the researcher determines how they will manage demographic material and transcripts. In addition, the researcher typically establishes and prepares a coding team.

https://doi.org/10.1037/0000408-005
Essentials of Constructivist Critical Incident Technique, by H. L. Schwartz and E. L. Holloway

Organizing the Data

First, the researcher develops processes for tracking demographic material and managing and coding transcripts. The most efficient way to organize demographic material is to create a spreadsheet with column headings that reference each attribute. For example, a log may include participant names, pseudonyms, interview dates, pertinent demographic data, contact information, receipt of informed consent, and receipt of the approved transcript. This file should be kept in a secure digital folder accessible only by the primary researcher.

Next, the researcher selects a system for managing and coding transcripts. Some researchers prefer the more kinesthetic paper-and-pencil approach. However, many now choose *computer-assisted qualitative data analysis software* (CAQDAS), which is a general term used to describe coding and textual analysis digital tools. Specific CAQDAS options available at the time of this writing include Dedoose and NVivo.

Of note, even when researchers use CAQDAS, they code transcripts manually within the application (as opposed to using an automated coding feature). Although some students are reluctant to devote the time needed to learn a new application (which may include training and accessing online support videos), we encourage them to make this investment because CAQDAS will ultimately save time (e.g., offering the potential to search for all passages related to a specific code) and provide analytic tools such as the ability to check codes in relation to demographic material. When we teach students how to code, we initially encourage them to code on paper or in a word-processing application (using the comment function) so they can pay attention to the coding process separate from learning new software. Then, with a sense of how to code, they engage in CAQDAS training.

We choose among CAQDAS options based on several features, including (a) secure storage of the project data to meet institutional review board (IRB) requirements; (b) the ability to back up projects on one's hard drive; (c) the capacity for the project to be viewed, coded, and edited by multiple coders as approved by the IRB; and (d) the ability to group and regroup data based on participant and incident attributes. When recommending CAQDAS options, we also consider costs and learning curves associated with various programs.

As noted previously, in CIT studies, the unit of analysis is the incident and not the participant. Participants will report multiple incidents; consequently, one interview will include several units of analysis, which has implications for setting up the project in CAQDAS. First, before uploading the transcript, cut and paste each incident into a new document so each uploaded document includes only one incident. Untangling one incident from another may be difficult, as participants may share incidents as part of a storyline even though the interview structure is designed to identify separate incidents. Researchers who encounter this complexity may wish to consult their coding team, faculty advisor, or co-researcher for support in separating incidents.

Second, establish a naming convention for the documents prior to uploading them in a CAQDAS program. Typically, a pseudonym and an incident number are used (e.g., Steph1, Steph2, Steph3, Steph4, Jake1, Jake2, and so on). After you upload an incident, use the CAQDAS attribute function to attach demographic data to each transcript (this will make more sense when you are working in CAQDAS).

Forming and Preparing a Coding Team

In our research, we work with a coding team to deepen our understanding of the data and help establish trustworthiness. The researcher's decision regarding whether to use a coding team likely depends on that person's views of interpretivism. Scholars who believe the researcher should be the sole interpreter will forego a coding team. While we embrace the researcher's interpretive role, we concurrently believe that a coding team can help the primary researcher expand their understanding of the data and moderate their own meaning-making so as to avoid overriding that of the participants. Further, we find that novice researchers who are still developing their coding skills benefit from working with a team. Finally, student researchers will consider program norms and expectations when deciding on the potential role of a team.

We have initiated a pay-it-forward culture in our graduate program, in which we invite students learning CIT to participate in coding in an ongoing CIT dissertation. In this way, students can learn and practice coding and become more familiar with the method as they prepare for their dissertation. This culture of collaboration has also led many of our alumni to serve on other students' dissertation coding teams for the pleasure of giving back to those who follow.

The topic of the study influences the composition of the coding team. Typically, in addition to the primary researcher, a team includes two or three members with varied backgrounds and experiences (a range of worldviews brings a richer analytical understanding to the data). Ideally, in studies including participants from historically marginalized groups, the team should include at least one member with a similar cultural or social identity if the primary researcher is not of the culture; although this person cannot represent an entire group, they can at least bring their own perspective to the work. In instances where it is impossible to have such a collaborator join the coding team, we ask an individual who is a member of the culture to consult in reviewing the interpretive process as the analysis progresses. Cultural consultants may be reimbursed for their contribution and, if they consent, acknowledged in the manuscript. Although we offer this guidance, we remind researchers that, from an intersectional perspective, one must be deeply thoughtful and critically reflexive when considering research with a community that is not one's own. Given the history of outsiders researching communities that are underrepresented and then committing ethical breaches—from voyeuristic drop-ins to benefitting from a community's intellectual resources without attribution or compensation—the entitled actions of researchers with privilege have a problematic and harmful legacy (Esposito & Evans-Winters, 2022).

In constructivist CIT, we treat the coding process as an interpretive endeavor that relies on group discussion to consider participants' meaning. This approach has been referred to as *dialogical intersubjectivity* (Saldana, 2013) and depends on team discussion of codes and the meaning coders infer from the excerpts. Simple consensus is a goal when passages raise a multitude of meanings; however, in situations where consensus cannot be achieved, the primary researcher makes the final adjudication. Because the team approach demands considerable time and collective decision making, members must be committed to the project, open to considering diverse opinions, and prepared to work cooperatively.

Preparing and guiding a coding team for a constructivist CIT project involves several steps.

1. At the first meeting, team members introduce themselves and describe their cultural and social background, professional background, and interest in being on the team. The primary researcher describes the purpose of the study, methodology, research questions, and requirements for confidentiality. Team members are encouraged to reflect on the research agenda and discuss their experience, presuppositions, and emotional responses to the topic.

2. Some team members may not be familiar with constructivist CIT coding. In this case, the supervising faculty member or someone else knowledgeable in the process provides training for the team.

3. Members of the coding team, in consultation with the primary researcher, decide whether to code in CAQDAS, in a word-processing application, or on paper. If they choose to use CAQDAS, the primary researcher will

establish unique project spaces for each member of the team within the software. The principal researcher has control over the primary copy of the project.

We emphasize that each coding team member must store and work on transcripts in their own project space and not in the primary project; otherwise, the principal researcher will have to delete all multiple codes and do an overwhelming amount of editing in their central workspace (this will make sense once you are familiar with CAQDAS). Coding team members who do not know how to use or do not have access to CAQDAS may code using the comment function in their word-processing application or on paper.

CODING

We begin this section by exploring coding as it is generally understood in qualitative research. Then we discuss coding approaches in the context of constructivist CIT.

What Is Coding?

A *code* in qualitative analysis is a word or phrase used to capture the meaning of a message in discourse. Charmaz (2006) considers the process of coding as a *critical link* between gathering textual data and conducting the analytical process. Saldana (2013) described a code as "most often a word or short phrase that symbolically assigns a summative, salient, essence-capturing, and/or evocative attribute for a portion of language-based or visual data" (p. 3).

In the qualitative literature, methodologists use myriad labels to describe coding steps and types of codes in textual analysis. Although many methodologies, such as grounded theory and narrative analysis, offer standard language to describe coding structures, no systematic description of coding processes in constructivist CIT currently exists. To bring consistency to the coding labels and processes of constructivist CIT analysis, we present a protocol identifying various types of coding and their functions. We review this protocol in the following sections (also see Table 5.1).

Constructivist CIT Coding Overview

In constructivist CIT, we engage in two types of coding for each transcript: structural and emergent (see Table 5.1). Structural coding is the first step after the transcript is prepared and uploaded to a CAQDAS program. Constructivist

TABLE 5.1. Constructivist Critical Incident Technique Coding Nomenclature

Code type	Label	Description
Structural coding	Types of incidents	Incidents broadly classified according to their nature
	Antecedent-incident-outcome (A-I-O)	Portions of an incident classified as antecedent, incident, or outcome
	Positive or negative, helped or hindered	Incidents classified according to their influence
Emergent coding	Descriptive codes	Paraphrases of a passage of the interview in a word or short phrase
	In vivo	Participant words or short phrases used as descriptive codes
	Indigenous	Codes representing specific words or expressions unique to a culture, language, or community
	Process	Gerunds describing actions, social processes, or psychological processes
	Categorical codes	Terms or concepts used to represent related descriptive codes; these become categories
	Subcategories	Categories become subcategories when clustered under broader conceptual terms

CIT researchers employ structural coding to identify components of the incident (antecedent, incident, and outcome [A-I-O]) as well as the incident type. The term *structural coding* may not be familiar to researchers who are adept with qualitative methods other than CIT. We refer to this aspect of coding as structural because the purpose is to identify and label structural components of each incident—in other words, to label incidents by virtue of their nature. This coding process enables constructivist CIT-specific types of analysis later in the process. The identification of structural elements (A-I-O) has been used in qualitative CIT analysis; here, we are giving it a label that differentiates CIT and constructivist CIT from other qualitative coding nomenclature.

Emergent coding includes descriptive and categorical coding. We refer to this aspect of coding as emergent to signal that the researcher develops these codes based on language and meaning shared by participants, rather than assigning codes from a previously developed coding taxonomy. Emergent coding is constructivist and sits on the interpretivist continuum. The researcher co-constructs meaning as they engage with the participant's own meaning-making. And while we encourage researchers to stay close to participant language and privilege participant perspective above their own, making sense of another's world is always an interpretive process. As noted earlier, standpoint epistemology affirms that we cannot help but to see the world through our own perspective.

Before we deepen our consideration of structural and emergent coding, we want to respond to a frequent question from students: "Do I wait until all the interviews are completed before I start coding?" In constructivist CIT designs, incident count, typically combined with saturation, determines sample size. To use saturation as a guide in sampling, a constant comparison approach to coding is required. As mentioned previously, the researcher interviews and then codes in an iterative process (Figure 3.1), noting emergent themes along the way and then interviewing additional participants until significant themes are richly detailed. For example, as Viscione (2022) reflects on what became an overarching theme (being the first and only), she captures part of her constant comparison process in a memo (Box 5.1). Note that after she recognizes the theme, she returns to earlier interviews and explores whether the theme is also reflected in those transcripts. Additionally, she holds theme awareness as she conducts future interviews. Viscione's description of her process powerfully illustrates this movement between past and future interviews and coding—the dynamic constant comparative process.

After the first few interviews, the researcher might do a few more interviews in a row before coding, but we recommend never more than three. If the researcher completes an extended stretch of interviews without keeping pace with coding, they are no longer engaged in constant comparison and diminish the opportunity to discover emerging themes and determine

---

BOX 5.1

ANALYTIC MEMO ILLUSTRATING THE CONSTANT COMPARISON PROCESS

The overarching themes became evident after the first 10 interviews. It was [in] interview #8 that [the participant] insisted being the first or only was an incident. I pushed back and insisted on her sharing a specific incident as in what happened. She said the condition repeated continuously and it/the condition was the most critical and was most definitely the most impactful critical incident across her career. That conversation had me review all my interviews and it presented more than once in each interview. Going forward I was more aware when [the term] first or only was mentioned.

saturation. In the following sections, we deepen our coding conversation, exploring how to engage in structural and emergent coding.

Structural Coding

As noted earlier, structural coding includes coding for incident type and coding portions of incidents as antecedent, incident, and outcome. Each is described next.

Coding for Incident Type

The first step in structural coding is to review incidents to confirm their alignment with the study design. Incidents not relevant to the topic are set aside. In our study of professor and student interactions (Schwartz & Holloway, 2014), we confirmed that all incidents were between professors and students (and would have excluded incidents between students, for example).

Then, we engaged in classifying incidents by type, which is the next step in structural coding. Classifying incidents by type is an emergent process in which the classification scheme is based on the data collected rather than on theory-driven incident types. This is an empirical, data-driven process as the researcher sees clusters of incidents that are similar, names each cluster, and begins to identify variations within each cluster. For example, after the first few interviews in our study, we determined that the general topic of the interaction and the location in which it occurred were distinguishing characteristics (Schwartz & Holloway, 2014). So, we coded each incident by type (academic, academic writing, future planning, or personal) and by incident setting (in class, before or after class, outside of class [e.g., the professor's office], phone or email, or nonacademic informal interactions [e.g., campus social events]). This process confirmed that the study sample was relevant to the typical situations in which professors and students engage, adding credibility and transferability to the study's findings. Not all studies will have the range or level of specific characterization of incidents as in our study; however, incidents are reviewed for their relevance to the overall purpose of the study. In some studies, clear incident types do not emerge and this naming structure is not used in reporting the study.

Coding Antecedent, Incident, and Outcome

The constructivist CIT researcher is interested in discovering, from the participant's perspective, the situation or conditions that evoked the incident (sometimes named the incident's antecedents) and the incident's consequences, influence, or outcomes. Thus, the next coding step involves labeling large portions of the incident as antecedent, incident, and outcome (often abbreviated as ANT, INC, or OUT for coding purposes). As discussed in Chapter 4, constructivist CIT interviews are designed to focus the participant on relaying specific incidents in which antecedents to the incident and subsequent impacts are readily evident. However, given the way in which some participants share incidents, the A-I-O demarcation may be less clear. For example, an outcome of one incident might be the antecedent to another incident. Similarly to when researchers have difficulty separating incidents, A-I-O coding is sometimes challenging, and we again encourage researchers to consult with their coding team, faculty advisor, or co-researcher.

Researchers who intentionally seek positive and negative events (or some other binary structure, such as helped and hindered) will also code each incident according to this framework. Structural coding allows you to search the project in CAQDAS by incident type and A-I-O. This search capability will become important when you are analyzing the data, allowing you to locate and review transcript excerpts that support various themes and theoretical ideas, find exemplary excerpts you may wish to quote in the manuscript, and cross-review coded excerpts with attributes (i.e., tags that serve to attach demographic data to each transcript). For example, this functionality allowed us to determine connections between incident type and location (Holloway & Schwartz, 2014).

Emergent Coding

In emergent coding, coders look for the meaning of participants' messages and choose language to represent the meaning, assigning a few words to a line or passage in the transcript. In a simple example, a participant describes feeling "motivated" after meeting with her mentor to discuss her thesis idea; depending on the context, we might code this as "feeling motivated." Charmaz (2002) suggests naming these codes with *gerunds* (verbs ending in -ing) to capture action and reflect the dynamic aspect of the experience. Although coders will necessarily filter meaning through their subjective understanding, they are actively mindful of their positions and perspectives and seek as much as possible to represent participant meaning rather than their own views. One of the key strategies in this endeavor is to use participant words when possible. So, in the previous example, a coder, remembering the participant's tone, might consider coding the passage "feeling inspired," however, by coding it as "feeling motivated," the coder sets aside their own interpretation and honors the participant's chosen words. Nonetheless, none of us can entirely supersede our experiences and mental models, and the importance of multiple coders with different worldviews plays a critical role in the trustworthiness of emergent coding. While engaging in emergent coding, we also use the memo function in CAQDAS to capture powerful quotes that we might wish to use later in the study report (see your CAQDAS user materials to learn this function). Researchers who choose not to use CAQDAS may memo in a digital or paper document. We encourage memoing in a digital document, as the researcher can later search the document quickly throughout the analytical process and when writing the manuscript.

In the following section, we discuss five types of emergent coding: descriptive, in vivo, indigenous, process, and categorical (see Table 5.1). We also describe the role of coding within each approach.

Descriptive Coding

Descriptive coding strives "to bring meaning, structure, and order to the data" (Anfara, 2008, p. 932). In descriptive coding, coders select passages that reflect participants' thinking, emotion, actions, and descriptions of the incident. The coder chooses descriptive words or phrases that characterize the primary meaning of the passage selected. These codes are referred to as *descriptive codes*. At this stage of the process, coders should avoid making interpretive leaps by applying conceptual codes and should instead generate codes that reflect participants' descriptions of their experiences.

In Vivo Coding

In vivo codes stick particularly close to the participant's language and retain participant meaning and nuance. For example, coders should be attentive to unique phrases, metaphors, or references that are significant in meaning and code these instances using the phrases or words used by the participant; these types of codes are named *in vivo codes*.

Indigenous Coding

Indigenous codes are in vivo codes that are culturally specific. Indigenous coding is especially important as participants are members of subcultures and identity groups. Words, phrases, and expressions may be unique to the culture and hold significant meaning in the participants' lived experiences.

Process Coding

According to Saldana (2013), codes that refer to "simple observable activities (e.g., reading, playing, watching TV, drinking coffee) and more general psychological or cognitive activity (e.g., struggling, negotiating, surviving, adapting) can be coded as such through a process code" (p. 96). Process codes are significant in constructivist CIT because they often describe the central activity of the critical incident and are influenced by and influence the antecedent and outcome.

Emergent coding generates numerous codes quickly. As the primary researcher, you have the task of recognizing, organizing, trimming, and reorganizing the descriptive codes. We refer to this as *cleaning the codes*: it is a process of tidying the collection of codes, without sacrificing meaning, so the developing code structure is more coherent and manageable. Researchers look for and resolve spelling errors, variations in tenses, similar codes with minimal discrepancy in the language, and other variations that lead to different codes with the same meaning. For example, a project might contain three different codes that due to tenses and a spelling error (feeling motivated, felt motivated, felling motivated) could be combined into one. We recommend cleaning the codes every few interviews. Although this might seem like busywork, it will make your overall process much more efficient and is part of the iterative loop depicted in Figure 3.1.

Categorical Coding and Subcategories

Once you have a clean set of codes, you will notice common characteristics among some codes. After the first few interviews, you will take a further step in cleaning the codes—that is, clustering them together under a new term or category. This clustering of codes is called *categorical coding*. As you continue clustering codes under categories, you may find that you have subcategories that describe a subset of the codes within the category. For example, imagine you have codes such as oranges, lemons, peaches, and plums. You group these codes under the category of fruit. You also notice that you have citrus fruit and stone fruit within the fruit category, so you name these subcategories and place the individual fruits under the appropriate subcategory with their descriptive codes under the overarching category, fruit. You have created a three-level, hierarchical coding structure, sometimes referred to as a *coding tree* (Saldana, 2013, p. 11).

Engaging the Coding Team

Consider the following five steps for engaging the coding team.

1. When the primary researcher has completed their first interview and prepared the transcript, the team process begins. All coders code one participant's incidents independently. The primary researcher then reviews all coded incidents side-by-side, looking for discrepancies. The primary researcher sometimes sees something new in team members' coding that resonates and they adjust their own coding in accordance, resolving the discrepancy. Next, the primary researcher meets with the coding team to discuss remaining inconsistencies. Again, from a constructivist perspective, this is an interpretive process; there are no right or wrong codes

and, consequently, teams typically reach consensus through dialogue. As an interpretivist, the primary researcher can legitimately make a final decision as they hold the fuller context of the study.

2. At this stage, coding team members begin to take on more transcripts without needing to meet after each one. Coders are progressively given three incidents to code independently. The primary researcher then reviews the coded transcripts and repeats the process described in Step 1.

3. By this point, the primary researcher begins to see more alignment between their own codes and the team members' and coders work more independently. Coders are given incidents from three different participants (this typically equals between nine and 12 incidents). One participant's incidents are given to all team members and then each team member also has incidents from two other participants (not given to other team members). Knowing that one of the participant's incidents will be coded by others on the team, but not knowing which set of incidents it is, may help team members stay focused and avoid coding fatigue.

4. The primary researcher reviews the codes on transcripts coded by team members. The primary researcher again looks for discrepancies and repeats the process described earlier.

5. At this point, prior engagement with the coding team and their work has helped the primary researcher refine their ability to stay close to participant meaning-making while coding, so the coding team may begin to take on a reduced role. Most team members stop actively working on the project, although one person, sometimes thought of as the research buddy, remains involved. Keep in mind that constructivist CIT is an interpretive process and the primary researcher is ultimately responsible for the interpretation of the data. Reduced engagement by the coding team is common in interpretive methodologies (Clandinin, 2007; Saldana, 2013; Smith et al., 2022). In constructivist CIT, the primary researcher legitimately moves forward with less coding team involvement; however, they actively confer with the remaining team member for feedback and consultation regarding coding and other aspects of this interpretive work.

THEMATIC ANALYSIS

Several interviews into the study, you will begin to see larger conceptual ideas or themes and, at this point, you have begun thematic analysis, the analytic process (Braun & Clarke, 2021). You begin to identify conceptual ideas or *themes* that combine categories under one label. In this phase, you strive to represent and interpret meaning conveyed across participants' experiences by more conceptual, interpretive labeling of themes. This itera-tive process reduces the number of categories, as codes are clustered and merged until essential categories are grouped to form larger conceptual themes. During this process, analytical memoing is important for recording and developing your thinking as you build a conceptualization of critical inci-dents and the participants' lived experiences. Inevitably, not all categories will fit into the primary themes identified and some will be set aside as outliers; however, the intent is to choose themes that are significant across incidents and respond to the research questions. If novice researchers find this stage of analytical work difficult inside CAQDAS, we encourage them to make sticky notes of emergent themes and arrange the notes on a large surface per their relation or relevance to one another.

As we identify categories or even incidents that otherwise do not fit the primary emergent themes, we consider them outliers and ask what else they tell us and how they may help us more fully develop our understanding of the studied phenomenon. For example, in our study regarding faculty and student interactions (Schwartz & Holloway, 2014), most reported incidents were positive in nature. However, one participant reported two negative inci-dents. We classified these as outlier incidents, analyzed them, and included them in the final report, thus adding a further dimension to the findings. As noted in Chapter 2, outlier incidents may contribute to credibility by bring-ing forward voices that are otherwise marginalized. In addition, knowing there is a place in the reporting for incidents that seem important but do not otherwise fit emerging themes gives the researcher an option to retain these incidents in the study without forcing thematic fit, supporting confirmability. Finally, outlier incidents may suggest areas for future research.

Revisiting Themes Within the A-I-O Structure

The next task is to consider themes relevant to the unfolding of critical incidents—that is, the positioning of themes in the context of antecedents, incidents, and the impact or outcome on the person and situation. The themes are placed under one of three columns: antecedents or conditions, the incident, and outcomes. We ask students to focus first on themes that represent the action of the incident and to place these themes under the center (incident) column. As we noted earlier, these themes are often expressed as gerunds and tend to emerge from process codes. Once the primary themes describing the incidents are placed, the antecedents and impacts are situated under their respective columns. The result is a depiction of incident patterns from left to right across the columns.

In our study regarding meaningful interactions between students and pro-fessors, for example, we considered themes in relation to the A-I-O framework and this informed both theory and practice (Schwartz & Holloway, 2014). Themes identified as antecedents centered relational conditions that were precursors to meaningful interactions. These relational conditions included students sensing that faculty members welcomed student interaction and that professors respected or were excited about the student's work. Themes that formed the actual meaningful actions (or critical events) included various kinds of teaching interactions, such as sharing resources and clarifying course material. Finally, themes that illustrated outcomes included the ability to move forward on assignments and scholar identity development. These examples illustrate how working in the A-I-O framework allowed us to see connections with the mentoring episodes construct (from the relational cultural theory literature) and informed recommendations for practice as we united four overarching themes and then categorized the cluster as "individualized attention," an approach faculty can take to encourage meaningful interactions with students.

Keep in mind that the A-I-O review is not a reaggregation process: You are not actually rebuilding literal incidents, so you are not likely to see single A-I-O progressions. Rather, this process provides an overview of the kinds of antecedents, incidents, and outcomes found in the study. Box 5.2 presents an excerpt from Viscione's (2022) A-I-O review.

BOX 5.2

CRITICAL INCIDENT TECHNIQUE ANTECEDENTS, CRITICAL INCIDENTS, AND OUTCOMES WITH EMERGENT CODES

Antecedents	Critical incidents	Outcomes
Good boss	Unexpected opportunity emerged (serendipity)	Promotion to next level/ increase in pay
Affinity network engagement	Plateaued in career/ passed over	Increased political savvy; awareness of unwritten expectations, rules, and processes
Not welcomed/ not invited/ outsider status	Confronted inappropriate behavior/lack of support	Sadness/anger/frustration/ exhaustion
Strong faith/full of optimism	Broadened skill set	Changed employer/moved to self-employment

Examining Themes in Relation to Attributes

In some CIT studies, researchers seek to compare themes within incident types or across demographic characteristics. For example, in our study of mentoring moments, we examined the type of incident in relation to major themes from the emergent coding. We thought that different types of incidents might correspond with a particular theme. For example, did students report out-of-classroom interactions as focused on personal rather than academic topics? Because all incidents had been typed in the first round of analysis, we had the means to examine themes within incident type. The specific steps in this type of cross-comparison analysis can be found in the original report (Schwartz & Holloway, 2014). In Chapter 6, we explore approaches for deepening the analysis.

6 DEEPENING THE ANALYSIS

In this chapter, we continue to describe the analytical process, including theory building, consulting with others during later stages of the study, and visual modeling. Refer to Figure 3.1 to follow this process.

TOWARD THEORY BUILDING

As noted in Chapter 1, researchers in a range of disciplines have recognized the capacity of the critical incident technique (CIT) for building theory that is relevant and meaningful to practice (Woolsey, 1986). Theory building begins during the coding process.

Emergent coding relies on coders' inductive process as they use their natural capacity to make sense of a situation. At a higher level of conceptualization, the researcher begins to see multiple new connections within the coding structure. As the researcher lets go of previously held assumptions about the phenomenon, they likely recognize novel patterns that shed new light on the experience described by study participants. These cognitive processes represent *abductive thinking*—a cognitive capacity to make leaps of

https://doi.org/10.1037/0000408-006
Essentials of Constructivist Critical Incident Technique, by H. L. Schwartz and E. L. Holloway

understanding through imagining new ways of seeing the data. This conceptual work establishes a more abstract understanding that goes beyond the specific descriptive perspective of the study and enhances the transferability of the key findings. An excellent description of the process by which theory emerges from thematic analysis of qualitative data is provided in Saldana (2013, p. 250). In summary, creating novel and meaningful conceptualizations of the situation begins theory building.

Working with the data, for example, Viscione (2022) saw a connection among several beliefs expressed by participants. She conceptualized these as "sustaining beliefs," which became an overarching theme:

> The second overarching theme—sustaining beliefs shared by the participants— was also core to the career advancement experience. The three sustaining beliefs expressed with regularity by the participants were having a strong faith or spirituality, having a strong sense of self-worth, and the belief that women leaders and Black leaders should support each other. These beliefs were expressed explicitly and implicitly. (Viscione, 2022, p. 99)

Given that the researcher is working with findings from one study, they will not put forth a fully articulated theory but may develop a preliminary, substantive, or middle-range theory (Timmermans & Tavory, 2012). This preliminary theory may inform practice and serve as a starting point for future studies. Not all studies break new theoretical ground, and novice researchers should not think that this diminishes their work. Findings that offer language for previously unnamed and tacitly understood experiences can affirm and inform practice. For example, Viscione (2022) stated the following:

> The final finding was another that I had some subconscious awareness of, but it was not front of mind related [to] the career advancement of Black women. This was the frequency of being new—in an organization, a position, a level, or a geography—contributed to what the participants identified as most impactful career advancement incidents. I knew from my previous work experience that it was not advisable to have more than two new change dimensions in a career change. What I had not considered was the possible differences experienced by single or double minorities in managing the changes related to expectations, new cultures, new people, learning new work, and all the other transitions required in organizations that are raced and gendered when there are very few people that look like you. This is exponential culture shock. My insights and learnings were many and it is my hope that they will be helpful to others seeking to advance more Black women in Fortune 1000 companies. (pp. 177–178)

New conceptualizations of emergent patterns can offer unique perspectives of individual experience of critical occurrences in context and this can be significant, influencing practice, theory development, and future studies.

DEEPENING THE CONCEPTUAL WORK

In this section, we discuss the role and process of engaging others to further develop findings and theoretical ideas. We also describe the role of visual modeling in constructivist CIT.

Engaging Others Through the Analytical Process

The deep thinking required for good analytical work can be both joyful and, at times, an intellectual tangle. We have enjoyed the generative power of thinking together at literal and virtual dining room tables—whiteboard nearby, with ideas flowing. Likewise, we encourage students to engage with others during this process. There are moments when we, as researchers, see connections and want to talk them through with others to see if the logic holds. Other times, we have a sense that we cannot resolve a lingering category or seemingly unfinished concept, so we seek a dialogic process to clarify or expand our thinking. Although much of the research process can be solitary, we endorse collaborative conversations as sources of support and thinking together for conceptual clarity.

For guidance on identifying possible consultants, we encourage students to consider their research topic and context, their emerging ideas, and their own disposition. Our students often find value in convening their coding team to discuss findings, as the coding team brings familiarity with the data and overall study. In other cases, particularly as they work to sharpen the language of themes and preliminary theory, students may engage other student colleagues who were not previously involved in the study. These trusted peers often bring fresh energy and perspective, which helps the primary student researcher refine their thinking at this critical stage. In addition, students who hold each other in high regard bring appreciation for the primary researcher's work, and this can provide a meaningful boost late in the process.

Student researchers may also discuss their findings, including thorny conceptual problems as well as exciting discoveries, with their dissertation chair and methodologist, depending on the program culture and norms. We often enjoy thinking with our students at this stage of the work.

Finally, constructivist CIT researchers may take their findings back to participants for additional collaborative thinking and feedback. As another form of member checking, this is particularly important when the researcher is an outsider in relation to the studied population. Later-stage member checking can be an additional form of data collection and conceptual development if approached systematically (Esposito & Evans-Winters, 2022; Lucas et al., 2018).

Visual Modeling as an Analytical Process

A think display is suggested as a typical process for organizing themes and concepts as they relate to the research questions (Miles & Huberman, 1994; Miles et al., 2014). We often use graphic sketches throughout the analytical process to gain further insight into connections among concepts and make sense of the overall findings from a practice perspective. When we suggest this method to students, they sometimes reply, "I can't draw." So we clarify that this process can be akin to mind mapping in a most basic form—using the space of a visual field to position concepts in relation to each other (proximal or distal), indicating connections, and, when relevant, portraying a progression or some other dynamic relationship. We refer students and other researchers seeking to learn more about visual representation of qualitative data to relevant scholarly work, including Scagnoli and Verdinelli (2017), Verdinelli and Scagnoli (2013), and Watkins et al. (2022), as well as design resources such as three types of User Experience (UX) diagrams for visualizing qualitative data (Humble, 2023).

This early mind mapping often deepens our analytical thinking as it pushes us to review emergent conceptual ideas and sometimes surfaces new connections or constructions. In this phase, we are likely to continue the constant comparison process as we return to codes and coded passages to confirm our later conceptual thinking. We and our students often work through several iterations until we feel the visualization communicates the findings.

Viscione (2022) developed her visual model (Figure 6.1) with the intent of portraying the context (Black women executives in Fortune 1000 companies with 15-plus years of management experience), overarching themes (being the first and only and sustaining beliefs), and antecedents, incidents, and outcomes evident through the analysis. The graphic in the center clearly conveys the power of the overarching themes—being the first and only and sustaining beliefs surround and hold these women's experiences. The upper and lower text boxes present a concise overview of overarching themes and primary A-I-O patterns. Also note the power and dynamism evoked by Viscione's use of gerunds and her careful wordsmithing in the final naming of themes. Reflecting on her process, she recommended creating a central language document listing all A-I-O themes, which she used as a reference when writing and revising to maintain consistency throughout the process. In Figure 6.1, Viscione provides one example of CIT data visualization. For additional examples, we refer readers to Watkins et al. (2022).

Ultimately, the visual representation should include recognizable categories, themes, and patterns that are surfaced in the analytic process. Stated simply, language used in the visual representation should match the language used in the textual description so the reader is easily oriented. Likewise, the model,

FIGURE 6.1. Visual Representation of Viscione's Findings

Exploring the Career Advancement Experience of Black Women on their Journey to Executive Level in Large Companies

OVERARCHING THEMES

THE EXPERIENCE OF BEING THE FIRST AND/OR THE ONLY:
- Having her qualifications or credibility questioned
- Feeling isolated, invisible, and unwelcome
- Being aware that she is different from the others
- Feeling unsupported at work
- Experiencing racism and, or sexism
- Looking up and over and not seeing people like her
- Feeling empowered, accomplished, proud, hopeful, lonely, disappointed, or frustrated

SUSTAINING BELIEFS
- Having a strong faith or spirituality
- Having a strong sense of self-worth
- Believing Black people and women should support each other

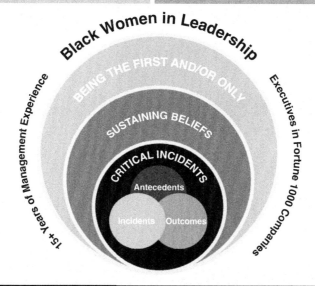

CRITICAL INCIDENT THEMES

ANTECEDENTS
- Being the first and/or only
- Having a strong faith or spirituality
- Being new in an organization, type of work, level, or position
- Experiencing strong support
- Feeling unsupported at work

INCIDENTS
- Building, maintaining, and leveraging critical relationships
- Broadening skills, insights, and experiences at level
- Leaving the company by choice or being forced out
- Experiencing racism and/or sexism
- Recognizing her career is off-track

OUTCOMES
- Gaining new skills, insights, and experiences
- Being promoted, pay increases, and new professional connections
- Experiencing stronger and different feelings about work
- Being more supportive of Black and women leaders
- Experiencing health concerns or issues
- Experiencing negative consequences that limit future career advancement

because of constructivist CIT's essential connection to practice, should have utility for practitioners in the field. Typically, we use the final visual model in the manuscript (and students share it in their dissertation defense). Many of our students have later used their models in teaching and training. Some researchers feel confident in their sketching skills or with a digital tool and create the final version for presentation. Others hire an artist or designer (or find a skilled family member or friend!) to create the final model.

7
WRITING THE MANUSCRIPT

Writing the manuscript provides researchers with an exciting opportunity to tell the story of their study. The story describes what inspired and informed the project (positionality and sensitizing concepts), the study framing and design, findings, theoretical ideas, and commitment to trustworthiness. Constructivist critical incident technique (CIT) researchers writing an article for journal submission should consult the journal's author guidelines and the American Psychological Association (APA) Journal Article Reporting Standards (JARS) for qualitative research (Levitt et al., 2018). If journal guidelines prohibit elements that seem central to qualitative work (e.g., first-person writing), we encourage you to identify a journal that more clearly supports qualitative research. If the journal appears to support qualitative work, then consult the journal submission guidelines for further guidance. Journal article manuscripts typically include an introduction, brief literature review, method overview (including a concise description of the methodology, rationale for choosing the method, participants, data collection, and analysis), findings, trustworthiness, and discussion.

For those using CIT in their dissertation, we offer the following encouragement. Students are often tired by the time they reach the final stages of

https://doi.org/10.1037/0000408-007
Essentials of Constructivist Critical Incident Technique, by H. L. Schwartz and E. L. Holloway

writing. We encourage them to engage in something that energizes them before writing the final chapter of the thesis or dissertation to finish strong. Ideally, both the energy and passion of the manuscript match the excitement that first motivated the study. The manuscript, whether a thesis, dissertation, or journal article, should itself have integrity. That is, the manuscript should have internal consistency, wherein descriptions and language are consistent and the findings, including quotes, tables, graphic representations, and composite narratives, are articulated such that all align in language and flow to integrate and support each other. To this end, we recommend developing and maintaining a document or spreadsheet with the names of all incident types and themes for use throughout the writing process.

CONSTRUCTIVIST CIT RHETORICAL STYLE

Several conventions guide researchers in writing the manuscript. Working through the constructivist CIT process, researchers necessarily move from full incidents to disaggregated pieces of data represented by codes and then to conceptual categories and themes. This disaggregation is essential in the emergent analytical process. However, to meaningfully share findings, we then need to convey the richness of significant incidents and a larger story of the studied phenomenon in context. The constructivist CIT researcher chooses among several approaches to tell the story of their findings, including participant quotes, visual models, and composite narratives.

Using Quotes

Constructivist CIT researchers, following the traditions of many qualitative methods, share quotes to support the articulation of themes and emerging theory and to center participant voices. Using quotes in the manuscript is an expected and important element of establishing trustworthiness, as readers should see clear connections among quotes, themes, and theoretical ideas. Selecting quotes for the final report can be energizing, as it helps the researcher engage once more with the participants' words, experiences, and emotions.

This part of the writing process also requires careful consideration as the researcher seeks to use quotes that illustrate themes and other findings while also bringing texture or subtlety to the page. Avoid using quotes that simply repeat what you have already written in describing a theme or other salient point, and instead use quotes that provide context, specificity, emotion, or in some other way illuminate the discussion. As a general practice, limit quotes to no more than five lines and use no more than two quotes to support a given theme or theoretical proposition. Novice researchers feeling rightfully energized by the power of participant words may be inclined to use longer and more frequent quotes; however, we believe that tempering the use of quotes strengthens the manuscript. First, the researcher's voice should provide the throughline for the paper. Second, overuse of quotes may result in a research report that remains descriptive while failing to communicate the researcher's analytical findings.

Illustrating Findings Visually and Through Composite Narratives

To decide whether to include visual modeling and composite narratives, consider how to best serve the study topic and findings, the texture of the incidents, the intended audiences, and your strengths and communication style. As noted in Chapter 6, we often engage in visual modeling to refine and represent findings. An effective visual model conveys significant material in a single space and should be a reference point, helping the reader make sense of the study.

Constructivist CIT researchers may also choose to create composite narratives. As Willis (2019) noted, "A composite narrative uses data from several individual interviews to tell a single story" (p. 471). Composite narratives are useful in qualitative research for reaggregating data to share findings, preserving confidentiality, and sharing findings with practitioner audiences (Willis, 2019). Using composite narratives calls on the researcher "to convey accurate, yet anonymized, portrayals of the accounts of a group of individuals" (Willis, 2019, p. 471). Creating a composite narrative, like developing a visual model, requires the researcher to reintegrate the material. This reintegration provides another opportunity for the researcher to engage deeply with the data, which may surface additional nuance in the findings.

Willis (2019) offers a process for creating composite narratives that can be applied to CIT. She advises drawing on three to five transcripts to create a narrative. Likewise, we suggest identifying key or overarching themes or incident types and then drawing on three to five incidents to create the narrative. Drawing on several incidents to create the narrative allows the researcher to portray significant incident types and themes while guarding participant anonymity. For detailed process and examples, please see Willis (2019).

Connecting With the Literature

As with many methods, constructivist CIT researchers situate their findings in the context of relevant literature. This process includes relating the findings to literature covered in the literature review. The discussion of findings may also lead the researcher to add and discuss literature not covered previously.

Scope of the Study

We believe that the constructivist philosophical foundations of constructivist CIT also point to another shift from conventional reporting—the section routinely called *limitations*. We typically advise students to articulate the *scope of the study*, rather than limitations (Lincoln & Guba, 1985). Too often, novice constructivist researchers, attempting to draft limitations, revert to the still-pervasive positivist mindset and, in so doing, undermine their own choice of methodology. For example, students will cite the reliance on participant self-report as a limitation when, in fact, this is a feature of constructivist CIT.

Framing this section as the study scope rather than its limitations shifts the focus to restating contextual and other factors that allow readers to determine transferability, further establishing trustworthiness. Scope may include elements such as geographic context, size or type of organizations represented by participants, and recency of incidents and related implications.

RETURNING TO TRUSTWORTHINESS

Finally, although space constraints in publication guidelines prohibit a lengthy exposition, constructivist researchers may include a final reflection on their experience conducting the study. This reflection brings the trustworthiness process full circle. In this space, the researcher may draw on material from their reflexive memos to share moments of awareness regarding their positionality. For example, Viscione shared observations regarding her experience with the research process (Box 7.1).

By providing a researcher reflection, the researcher enacts several trustworthiness criteria (Lincoln & Guba, 1985), including dependability (making the process transparent), confirmability (sharing their experience of centering participants' perspectives while acknowledging their own presence in the study), and transferability, as the reflection may help the reader continue to assess applicability of the findings in their context. In our experience, writing the researcher's reflection can be a meaningful experience, particularly for students as they name and articulate their struggles, growth areas, and excitement.

BOX 7.1
FINAL REFLEXIVE MEMO

My learning and insights were many and continuous. I found I needed to take breaks to process and incorporate my learning. I discovered that I loved the process of conducting research. I loved the organizing element of doing it. I am super curious and adventurous. I loved not knowing where it was going and repeatedly being surprised by the interview comments and patterns. There were quotes that caused me to stop in my tracks. The entire process was exciting to me. One of the areas where I learned most beyond my content focus was understanding and executing the role of the researcher. Throughout the dissertation process, my understanding of my role as a qualitative researcher grew exponentially. (Viscione, 2022, p. 172)

APA RESOURCES

Researchers will have likely used the most current edition of the APA publication manual (American Psychological Association, 2020b) when writing the study proposal and institutional review board materials. This manual will continue to be important for general writing and formatting guidelines.

We also refer students and others new to qualitative research to the APA JARS reported in Levitt et al. (2018). Levitt and colleagues described the JARS as follows: "This publication marks a historical moment—the first inclusion of qualitative research in APA style" (p. 26). They also confirmed the appropriateness and integrity of writing the study report in first person and explored essential elements of the qualitative manuscript, such as transparency and contextualization, to establish trustworthiness and potential transferability. The JARS provide novice qualitative researchers with language to articulate choices made in the qualitative domain (Levitt et al., 2018). This language and the weight of an APA statement can be particularly helpful when one encounters resistance from individuals who may be less familiar with qualitative methods (e.g., an external committee member or conference session attendee).

8

VARIATIONS ON THE METHOD

Although we have focused on constructivist critical incident technique (CIT) throughout much of this book, in this chapter we provide an overview of other CIT variations. These research designs use CIT as a foundation while incorporating features that enhance the exploration of participants' identification, understanding, and description of critical incidents. We include variations of qualitative CIT that are clearly described and well-established in the literature and offer elements that add significantly to traditional CIT approaches. These CIT variations include *enhanced critical incident technique* (ECIT), *sequential incident technique* (SIT), *switching path analysis technique* (SPAT), *criticality critical incident technique* (CCIT), and the *Critical Incident Questionnaire* (CIQ). We highlight adaptations that address specific research aims and contexts. In the following pages, we provide a brief overview of each variation to help researchers gain a sense of CIT's evolution and, when relevant, we highlight elements of the approach that align with and contribute to constructivist CIT.

https://doi.org/10.1037/0000408-008
Essentials of Constructivist Critical Incident Technique, by H. L. Schwartz and E. L. Holloway

ENHANCED CRITICAL INCIDENT TECHNIQUE

In 2005, Butterfield and colleagues from the University of British Columbia reviewed CIT's then-50-year history and noted its evolution from a task analysis method to one well-suited for "exploring personal experiences, psychological constructs, and emotions" (p. 485). They concluded that CIT lacked a coherent process for establishing credibility and trustworthiness. In response, they proposed ECIT as a much-needed and more structured approach to establishing rigor in CIT studies (Butterfield et al., 2005).

The framework of Butterfield et al. (2005) provides a postpositivist contrast to constructivist CIT's trustworthiness process. The authors proposed nine credibility checks, several of which engage independent consultation at specific stages of the process and seek to confirm various forms of validity. This framework became part of their variation on CIT, which is explicitly situated in a postpositivist epistemology (Butterfield & Borgen, 2005; Butterfield et al., 2005; McDaniel et al., 2020)

As noted in Chapter 3, ECIT introduced the wish-list question as a potential option for CIT interviews. Constructivist CIT researchers may adopt this ECIT strategy, asking participants to suggest people, information, and other resources that they believe could positively influence the studied situation. This question centers participants as experts and aligns powerfully with constructivist CIT.

SERVICE INDUSTRY VARIATIONS

Researchers in the service industry have developed several CIT variations that offer strategies that would be appropriate in a constructivist study and potentially add depth to data collection. Service industry researchers have used CIT variations to understand providers' relationships with customers, particularly customer motivation, rationale, and timing of decisions regarding whether to stay with or switch providers. These variations have significant potential to help constructivist CIT researchers explore other kinds of relationships in contexts including social services, education, and health care. Researchers of customer decision-making have offered three variations of import: SIT (Stauss & Weinlich, 1997), SPAT (Roos, 2002), and CCIT (Edvardsson & Strandvik, 2000; Roos, 2002). Each is discussed next.

Sequential Incident Technique

Hospitality industry researchers Stauss and Weinlich (1997) developed SIT to study the trajectory of customer relationships with a service provider.

They described this design as a process-oriented method and employed it to understand customers' perceptions of service delivery. SIT adds a strategy that could be employed in constructivist CIT, wherein the researcher seeks typical incidents, in addition to critical incidents, occurring sequentially over a relationship. In this design, researchers develop a service map of typical incidents. The map (a) traces interactions that occur chronologically in typical customer engagements and (b) asks participants to report on positive and negative critical incidents that may have happened during these specific engagements.

Stauss and Weinlich (1997) studied the following typical, yet specific touchpoints in customer reception: "guest passes through customs, transfer to the club-resort, arrival at club-resort, check-in, and the way to the hotel room" (p. 42). For each engagement along the customer path, the respondent was asked to describe what happened and whether they experienced any positive or negative episodes. This segmented approach to respondent's experience may work well when the relationship chronology is expected and predictable, such as a first-year college student moving through orientation day; however, it would be less compatible when the focus is on fluid and less predictable relationships, such as those in counseling and mentoring contexts.

Switching Path Analysis Technique

Roos (2002) developed SPAT as an adaptation of SIT to uncover the path leading to customers' decisions to leave a current grocery provider. She reasoned that the decision to terminate an existing relationship may be readily apparent, but the circumstance that led to the decision may not be evident. The SPAT purposeful sample (Roos, 1999) included participants who used a supermarket frequently and then switched to a different grocer; the sample did not include customers who remained with the initial store. The SPAT interviewer asked about not only the decision to switch and the resulting process but also how the participant felt about the switch and whether they would consider returning to the original supermarket. With this focus on the decision to cease a current service relationship, SPAT provided nuanced findings regarding why consumers shifted. "As the qualitative analysis showed, switching determinants were divided into three categories: the pushing determinant, the swayer, and the pulling determinant" (Roos, 1999, p. 79). SPAT can clearly be used beyond the retail context to explore decisions to end or switch to another provider or professional relationship. For example, SPAT may help researchers understand why people leave a job or discontinue treatment.

Criticality Critical Incident Technique

CCIT (Edvardsson & Strandvik, 2000), like SPAT, was developed to study customer decisions. Whereas SPAT is used to explore the conduct of switching providers and to retrospectively uncover the attributes that led to the decision, CCIT examines ongoing relationships and customers' intended behavior, focusing on incidents that customers consider critical in deciding whether to continue the service relationship. The CCIT design explores participant's judgment of an incident's degree of criticality—in other words, whether an incident is sufficiently egregious to influence the participant's judgment of the value of the relationship. Relationship endurance may affect the degree to which an event may be considered critical. For example, in a study of customer–provider relationships, an event such as missing a scheduled meeting, although a negative occurrence, may not be reported if it happened only once or twice in a long relationship. However, if there were no-shows at the beginning of a relationship or missed appointments were to occur repeatedly, this behavior might result in an unfavorable impression and a decision to end the relationship.

Although SIT, SPAT, and CCIT were developed to explore issues in service relationships, these variations are transferable to other domains where researchers seek to understand temporal dimensions and relational trajectories. One element to address is that in these variations, researchers provide a structure to help participants identify important phases of the experience as well as significant events within the phases. However, Fuglsang (2017) suggested that CIT interviews can be used to identify different phases in a process before proceeding with interviews that seek the experience individuals have in each phase. This approach may resonate for constructivists who resist study designs wherein the researcher frames elements of the encounter to be explored. Fuglsang's less structured approach opens the opportunity to draw on stakeholder understanding of critical phases of the situation, rather than defaulting to researcher or expert assumptions regarding what is essential.

CRITICAL INCIDENT QUESTIONNAIRE

CIT researchers employ open-ended questionnaires to collect critical incident data. CIQs have been widely used for data collection in health care (Cormack, 1983; Keatinge, 2002), hospitality (Hoffman & Chung, 1999), business (Berger et al., 2012), and coaching (Milner et al., 2013). Questionnaires provide a viable alternative when interviewing is not feasible or when study designs require a large sample. Although questionnaires lack the flex-ibility for follow-up questions, the structure of the questionnaire seeks to replicate traditional CIT questions and prompts such as these: "What hap-pened before the incident?" "What happened after the incident?" "What started (or ended) the incident?"

Perhaps the most well-known CIT-related questionnaire is Brookfield's CIQ. Brookfield (1998) advocated using this questionnaire weekly to invite stu-dent feedback. As noted in Chapter 1, Brookfield's CIQ prompts students to identify a range of moments in the week's class, focusing on five kinds of experiences—when the students felt engaged, distanced, affirmed or helped, confused, and surprised. Brandenburg and McDonough (2017) adapted Brookfield's CIQ for self-study in their teaching practices, exploring when they as teachers felt most engaged, distanced, surprised, affirmed, or helped by another teacher or student in their week of teaching. They recorded critical incidents in reflective journals and via questionnaires and email. Through this self-study, Brandenburg and McDonough identified critical incidents such as "being challenged by changing institutional structures and policies" (p. 229) and developed a more nuanced understanding of effective collaborations. Brandenburg and McDonough's adaptation and application of Brookfield's CIQ offers significant potential for self-study in numerous domains. We propose that critical incident reflection could serve as a fresh and more meaningful approach to workplace performance self-evaluations, thus giving employees and supervisors concrete experiences and related reflections to consider in both formative and summative assessments.

FUTURE APPLICATIONS

The adaptations to CIT provide innovative designs relevant to professionals who would benefit from identifying critical incidents in professional rela-tionships. For example, counseling, education, and leadership studies might consider activities that clients wished took place (wish-list items), the criti-cality of incidents in sustaining a relationship, or the critical incidents that led to termination of a relationship. In a constructivist CIT design, adapta-tions that focus on critical happenings in a relationship could also include perspectives from both the client and the provider, thus addressing Gremler's (2004) concern that there is an overemphasis on the examination of only one member of a dyadic relationship.

9
CONCLUSION

Seeking to reflect on our process before drafting this conclusion, we each identified and explored four meaningful moments we experienced while writing this book. Next, Harriet classified the incidents by type. Even in this informal critical incident reflection, we identified three incident types: writing, collaboration, and self-awareness. We share one of the incident types here. We both identified the same *collaborative* moment—working together on Zoom to clarify the coding language. Elizabeth reflected:

> Sitting across from you in Zoom struggling to get coding right, disagreeing with each other, unpacking our positions together, mindfully coming round to a decision, and then laughing at ourselves—that's the best!

Harriet recalled:

> The joy of doing challenging intellectual work together—moments where we resonated and moments where we saw things differently but worked through it with respect and openness. So cool to wrestle together with language and develop something we both believe in.

https://doi.org/10.1037/0000408-009
Essentials of Constructivist Critical Incident Technique, by H. L. Schwartz and E. L. Holloway

These excerpts reveal a sense of two people working through a difficult portion of the writing process. Each of us clearly experienced tension: Elizabeth recalled "disagreeing with each other," while Harriet noted "we saw things differently." Similarly, we both spoke of remaining connected through the process, Elizabeth remembered "unpacking our positions together," and Harriet claimed that it was "so cool to wrestle together with language." Notice the subtle differences in description and expression as we reflect on confronting and working through the dilemma. Commenting on qualities that helped the process, Elizabeth pointed to mindfulness, while Harriet named respect and openness. And we both indicated positive emotions, as Elizabeth remembered "laughing at ourselves" and Harriet recalled the "joy" of the experience. Contemplating these two recollections, we recognize underlying emotions that run beneath our collaborative process. In addition, we are energized by the potential of using constructivist critical incident technique (CIT) to explore dyadic relationships. We believe that if we continued this inquiry by further interrogating our language individually and together, the process would reveal more about how we manage differences in our relationship and energize each other in the work.

When we met to discuss the incidents, we intended to simply frame how we might use them in this concluding chapter. However, the dialogue evolved into a deeper conversation in which we further explored our individual and collaborative experiences, shared more about our understandings of ourselves in this process, and expressed some of what made this shared endeavor meaningful. This subsequent conversation reminded us that Gremler, as early as 2004 (pp. 78–79), suggested CIT might be applied to explore a dyadic perspective on an experience. From our brief sharing, we can imagine a constructivist CIT study that delves deeply into the meaning of collaboration in pairs. In addition, we see the power of studying multiple perspectives regarding shared critical incidents.

Throughout these pages, we have sought to convey our enthusiasm for CIT broadly and for constructivist CIT, in particular. We are confident that Viscione's (2022) work and other exemplar studies illustrate the method's power and potential. CIT is an established methodology with a deep history and continued growth in the social sciences and other domains, including health care and business management. Further, CIT studies hold potential for theory development, contribution to scholarly and practice discourses, and meaningful practice application. One of our intentions in writing this book is to promote CIT and constructivist CIT for increased recognition and presence among qualitative methodologies. Finally, we hope that this guide encourages and supports you as you consider and potentially conduct a critical incident study.

We conclude by reviewing the benefits and advantages of constructivist CIT, considering its potential contributions, describing its scope, and pondering its future.

BENEFITS OF CIT

Constructivist CIT offers many of the same advantages as CIT and other variations as well as distinct strengths. First, we explore benefits shared by CIT as broadly understood and then we suggest contributions specific to constructivist CIT.

CIT and its variations feature an inherent intuitiveness, making the methodology particularly accessible. Consider your own stand-out moments in relationships and important life experiences. For example, what were meaningful moments in your journey as a student? What have been turning points in an important friendship? When in the last week did you feel supported in school or at work? Identifying and reflecting on significant moments helps us make sense of our discrete experiences as well as the trajectory of our lives, including how we navigate challenges, see our growth, and deepen our understanding of self. Thus, the essence of CIT—critical moments—is part of routine sense-making in everyday life.

From a pragmatic perspective, CIT also holds several advantages. This methodology offers a solid blend of structure and flexibility, as noted throughout these chapters. Finally, faculty and students considering a CIT approach for advanced undergraduate, master's, and doctoral work can adjust the scope of the study to fit relevant timelines and expectations. For example, an undergraduate student might conduct a pilot CIT study with a limited number of participants, rather than work to saturation.

Specific Contributions of Constructivist CIT

We believe that constructivist CIT, as a clearly articulated variation, offers a significant step forward for the methodology. CIT has evolved throughout its history, particularly since the late 1990s, which may be seen as the start of a juncture in its advancement. In one methodological move, researchers including Chell (1998, 2014) and Ellinger and Bostrom (2002) moved in a constructivist direction. Later, Butterfield and colleagues (Butterfield et al., 2005; McDaniel et al., 2020) established ECIT, a postpositivist framework. Researchers from various disciplines have contributed to this constructivist shift, and we hope that constructivist CIT now provides a comprehensive framework that is philosophically sound, rich in detail for application, and still flexible such that it will have relevance across sectors. Moreover, in multimethod studies in which CIT is used with qualitative methodologies such as narrative analysis and phenomenology (Watkins et al., 2022), constructivist CIT brings coherence by providing methodological and trustworthiness processes that honor underlying interpretive epistemological stances typical of these other methods.

Constructivist CIT also places CIT more firmly in the contemporary qualitative landscape, aligning with the interpretive turn (Clarke, 2003) and an intersectional perspective (Esposito & Evans-Winters, 2022). First, constructivist CIT takes a decisive interpretivist stance, declaring that just as participants have a standpoint and cannot help but see the world through interpretation, so too do researchers; for researchers as well as participants, to think is to interpret. Constructivist CIT researchers acknowledge this as a reality and address implications through trustworthiness practices. Moreover, constructivist CIT centers participants and their perspectives throughout the study, from relying on their parsing of critical incidents and meaning-making to potentially engaging them in late-stage member checking—these practices correspond with interpretivist and intersectional stances.

Further, concurrent with intersectional approaches, constructivist CIT encourages researchers to commit to a social justice ethos, including benefit to communities that engage in research. Finally, constructivist CIT's trustworthiness process, which combines Lincoln and Guba's (1985) long-standing trustworthiness criteria with contemporary commitments to interrogating, articulating, and revisiting positionality in its many forms throughout the study (Dwyer & Buckle, 2009; Holmes, 2020; Jacobson & Mustafa, 2019; Kerstetter, 2012; Milner, 2007), reifies interpretivist, constructivist, and intersectional philosophies.

LIMITATIONS AND SCOPE

In Chapter 7, we recommended addressing scope rather than limitations when writing the study report. Likewise with this articulation of constructivist CIT, we resist the default practice of eliciting limitations of this technique and instead discuss scope. Limitations as a construct originated in positivist research and describe a study's weaknesses regarding reliability and validity, such as a small or otherwise limited sample, or confounding variables. We propose that the term *limitations* as used in positivist studies is meant to address the same questions as *trustworthiness* in interpretive studies (e.g., Is this study credible, and are these findings meaningful?); however, the translation does not work. The term limitations is treated as a convention to assess research universally; however, when qualitative researchers address limitations, they often default to a positivist framework and undermine their own choice of method. For instance, "small sample size" is often listed as a limitation of a qualitative method or study when, in fact, small sample size is an inherent feature of most qualitative studies that enables the kind of in-depth interviewing called for by the genre. Instead, we propose the term *scope* as a more appropriate and philosophically aligned approach to describing the range or capacity of the study. We believe that robust trustworthiness practices and description of scope address the questions intended when readers and reviewers of qualitative work inquire about limitations.

In this spirit, we review the scope of the methodology. Given CIT's focus on incidents or moments, the methodology is not a good fit for those seeking to explore the full arc of stories. Likewise, CIT requires researchers to work with incidents as the unit of analysis, so those who wish to consider individual experience and meaning-making by keeping people's stories intact may find other methods more suitable. However, among qualitative methods, CIT is unique in affording researchers a process by which to study incidents or moments that stand out in a given week or over the course of a project, career, or lifetime.

When employed with a solid study plan, deep and ongoing commitment to trustworthiness, and clear articulation of choices regarding terminology and implementation, CIT situates researchers to effectively explore the human experience by centering how people understand themselves and their world (Butterfield et al., 2005; Cardwell et al., 2020; Chell, 1998, 2014; Viscione, 2022; Woolsey, 1986). In addition, CIT is useful in studying process problems and effectiveness (Alobo et al., 2021; Flanagan, 1954) and for self-study (Brandenburg & McDonough, 2017; Brookfield, 1998).

LOOKING TO THE FUTURE

As a dynamic methodology with a substantial foundation, CIT continues to evolve. We envision five areas with important growth potential. First, although we have aimed to bring intersectional and critical lenses to this articulation of constructivist CIT, we see this as a foundation for a more theoretically critical postmodern approach to CIT. Second, as proposed earlier, we believe that the temporal-focused variations, including SIT (Stauss & Weinlich, 1997), SPAT (Roos, 2002), and CCIT (Edvardsson & Strandvik, 2000), can be meaningfully applied outside the service industry, particularly in those disciplines wherein ongoing relationships are central to practice (e.g., education, counseling, health care, and leadership). Third, we encourage self-study CIT variations (Brandenburg & McDonough, 2017; Brookfield, 1998) as an engaging workplace self-assessment process for reflection and learning. Fourth, aligned with Gremler (2004), we advocate using constructivist CIT to explore multiple perspectives in collaborative and relational practices. Finally, we offer this book as a first attempt at a comprehensive articulation of constructivist CIT and invite others to build on and refine our work.

Appendix

EXEMPLAR STUDIES AND REVIEWS

Alobo, G., Ochola, E., Bayo, P., Muhereza, A., Nahurira, V., & Byamugisha, J. (2021). Why women die after reaching the hospital: a qualitative critical incident analysis of the "third delay" in postconflict northern Uganda. *BMJ Open, 11*(3), e042909. https://doi.org/10.1136/bmjopen-2020-042909

Bott, G., & Tourish, D. (2016). The critical incident technique reappraised. *Qualitative Research in Organizations and Management, 11*(4), 276–300. https://doi.org/10.1108/QROM-01-2016-1351

Butterfield, L. D., Borgen, W. A., Maglio, A. T., & Amundson, N. E. (2009). Using the enhanced critical incident technique in counselling psychology research. *Canadian Journal of Counselling, 43*(4), 265–282.

Chell, E., & Pittaway, L. (1998). A study of entrepreneurship in the restaurant and cafe industry: Exploratory work using the critical incident technique as a methodology. *International Journal of Hospitality Management, 17*, 23–32. https://doi.org/10.1016/S0278-4319(98)00006-1

Flanagan, J. C. (1954). The critical incident technique. *Psychological Bulletin, 51*(4), 327–358. https://doi.org/10.1037/h0061470

Gremler, D. (2004). The critical incident technique in service research. *Journal of Service Research, 7*(1), 65–89. https://doi.org/10.1177/1094670504266138

Kellogg, A. H., & Liddell, D. L. (2012). "Not half but double": Exploring critical incidents in the racial identity of multiracial college students. *Journal of College Student Development, 53*(4), 524–541. https://doi.org/10.1353/csd.2012.0054

Mathew, D., Nishikawara, R., Ferguson, A. O., & Borgen, W. A. (2023). Cultural infusions and shifting sands: What helps and hinders career decision-making of Indigenous young people. *Canadian Journal of Career Development, 22*(1), 6–18. https://doi.org/10.53379/cjcd.2023.345

Norman, I. J., Redfern, S. J., Tomalin, D. A., & Oliver, S. (1992). Developing Flanagan's critical incident technique to elicit indicators of high and low quality nursing care from patients and their nurses. *Journal of Advanced Nursing, 17*(5), 590–600. https://doi.org/10.1111/j.1365-2648.1992.tb02837.x

Philpot, R., Smith, W., Gerdin, G., Larsson, L., Schenker, K., Linnér, S., Moen, K. M., & Westlie, K. (2021). Exploring social justice pedagogies in health and physical education through critical incident technique methodology. *European Physical Education Review, 27*(1), 57–75. https://doi.org/10.1177/1356336X20921541

Watkins, K. E., Ellinger, A. D., Suh, B., Brenes-Dawsey, J. C., & Oliver, L. C. (2022). Further evolving the critical incident technique (CIT) by applying different contemporary approaches for analyzing qualitative data in CIT studies. *European Journal of Training and Development, 46*(7/8), 709–726. https://doi.org/10.1108/EJTD-07-2021-0107

Woolsey, L. K. (1986). The critical incident technique: An innovative qualitative method of research. *Canadian Journal of Counselling, 20*(4), 242–254.

References

Alobo, G., Ochola, E., Bayo, P., Muhereza, A., Nahurira, V., & Byamugisha, J. (2021). Why women die after reaching the hospital: A qualitative critical incident analysis of the 'third delay' in postconflict northern Uganda. *BMJ Open, 11*(3), e042909. https://doi.org/10.1136/bmjopen-2020-042909

American Psychological Association. (2017). *Ethical principles of psychologists and code of conduct* (2002, Amended June 1, 2010, and January 1, 2017). https://www.apa.org/ethics/code/index

American Psychological Association. (2020a). *Other research transparency standards and disclosures for journal articles.* https://www.apa.org/pubs/journals/resources/standards-disclosures#positionality-statements

American Psychological Association. (2020b). *Publication manual of the American Psychological Association* (7th ed.).

Andrews, T. (2012). What is social constructionism? *Grounded Theory Review, 11*(1), 39–46.

Anfara, V. A. (2008). Visual data displays. In L. M. Given (Ed.), *The SAGE encyclopedia of qualitative research methods* (Vol. 2, pp. 930–934). Sage.

Berger, K. W., Stratton, W. E., Thomas, J. G., & Cook, R. A. (2012). Critical incidents: Demand for short cases elicits a new genre. *Business Case Journal, 19*(1), 6–20.

Birks, M., Chapman, Y., & Francis, K. (2008). Memoing in qualitative research: Probing data and processes. *Journal of Research in Nursing, 13*(1), 68–75. https://doi.org/10.1177/1744987107081254

Bott, G., & Tourish, D. (2016). The critical incident technique reappraised. *Qualitative Research in Organizations and Management, 11*(4), 276–300. https://doi.org/10.1108/QROM-01-2016-1351

Bradburn, N. M., Huttenlocher, J., & Hedges, L. (1994). Telescoping and temporal memory. In N. Schwarz, S. Sudman, J. Huttenlocher, & L. Hedges (Eds.), *Autobiographical memory and the validity of retrospective reports* (pp. 203–215). Springer-Verlag. https://doi.org/10.1007/978-1-4612-2624-6_14

Bradbury-Jones, C., & Tranter, S. (2008). Inconsistent use of the critical incident technique in nursing research. *Journal of Advanced Nursing, 64*(4), 399–407. https://doi.org/10.1111/j.1365-2648.2008.04811.x

Brandenburg, R., & McDonough, S. (2017). Using critical incidents to reflect on teacher educator practice. In R. Brandenburg, K. Glasswell, M. Jones, & J. Ryan (Eds.). *Reflective theory and practice in teacher education* (Vol. 17, pp. 223–236). Springer, Singapore. https://doi.org/10.1007/978-981-10-3431-2_12

Braun, V., & Clarke, V. (2021). To saturate or not to saturate? Questioning data saturation as a useful concept for thematic analysis and sample-size rationales. *Qualitative Research in Sport, Exercise and Health, 13*(2), 201–216. https://doi.org/10.1080/2159676X.2019.1704846

Brookfield, S. (1998). Critically reflective practice. *Journal of Continuing Education in the Health Professions, 18*(4), 197–205. https://doi.org/10.1002/chp.1340180402

Brookfield, S. D. (n.d.). *Using the Critical Incident Questionnaire (CIQ)*. https://www.stephenbrookfield.com/critical-incident-questionnaire

Brooks, D. A. (2021). *Liner notes for the revolution: The intellectual life of Black feminist sound*. Belknap Press of Harvard University Press.

Buckner, T. M. (2012). *Engaging moments: Adult educators reading and responding to emotion in the classroom* [Doctoral dissertation, University of Georgia]. https://getd.libs.uga.edu/pdfs/buckner_terrie_m_201205_edd.pdf

Butterfield, L. D., & Borgen, W. A. (2005). Outplacement counseling from the client's perspective. *The Career Development Quarterly, 53*(4), 306–316. https://doi.org/10.1002/j.2161-0045.2005.tb00661.x

Butterfield, L. D., Borgen, W. A., Amundson, N. E., & Maglio, A.-S. T. (2005). Fifty years of the critical incident technique: 1954–2004 and beyond. *Qualitative Research, 5*(4), 475–497. https://doi.org/10.1177/1468794105056924

Butterfield, L. D., Borgen, W. A., Maglio, A. T., & Amundsen, N. E. (2009). Using the enhanced critical incident technique in counselling psychology research. *Canadian Journal of Counselling, 43*(4), 265–282.

Cardwell, M. E., Soliz, J., Crockett, L. J., & Bergquist, G. L. (2020). Critical incidents in the development of (multi)ethnic-racial identity: Experiences of individuals with mixed ethnic-racial backgrounds in the U.S. *Journal of Social and Personal Relationships, 37*(5), 1653–1672. https://doi.org/10.1177/0265407520906256

Charmaz, K. (2002). Qualitative interviewing and grounded theory analysis. In J. F. Gubrium & J. A. Holstein (Eds.), *Handbook of interview research: Context & method* (pp. 675–694). Sage.

Charmaz, K. (2006). *Constructing grounded theory*. Sage.

Charmaz, K. (2014). *Constructing grounded theory* (2nd ed.). Sage.

Chell, E. (1998). Critical incident technique. In C. Cassell & G. Symon (Eds.), *Qualitative methods and analysis in organizational research: A practical guide* (pp. 51–72). Sage.

Chell, E. (2014). The critical incident technique: Philosophical underpinnings, method and application to a case of small business failure. In E. Chell

& M. Karatas-Ozkan (Eds.), *Handbook of research on small business and entrepreneurship* (pp. 106–129). Edward Elgar. https://doi.org/10.4337/9781849809245.00015

Chell, E., & Pittaway, L. (1998). A study of entrepreneurship in the restaurant and café industry: Exploratory work using the critical incident technique as a methodology. *International Journal of Hospitality Management, 17*(1), 23–32. https://doi.org/10.1016/S0278-4319(98)00006-1

Chou, F., Kwee, J., Buchanan, M., & Lees, R. (2016). Participatory critical incident technique: A participatory action research approach for counselling psychology. *Canadian Journal of Counselling and Psychotherapy, 50*(1), 51–74.

Clandinin, D. J. (Ed.). (2007). *Handbook of narrative inquiry: Mapping a methodology.* Sage. https://doi.org/10.4135/9781452226552

Clarke, A. E. (2003). Situational analysis: Grounded theory mapping after the postmodern turn. *Symbolic Interaction, 26*(4), 553–576. https://doi.org/10.1525/si.2003.26.4.553

Cormack, D. (1983). *Psychiatric nursing described.* Churchill Livingstone.

Crenshaw, K. (2005). Mapping the margins: Intersectionality, identity politics, and violence against women of color. *Cahiers du genre, 39*(2), 51–82. https://doi.org/10.3917/cdge.039.0051

Creswell, J. W., & Poth, C. N. (2018). *Qualitative inquiry & research design* (4th ed.). Sage.

Denzin, N. K., & Lincoln, Y. S. (2011). *The SAGE handbook of qualitative research* (4th ed.). Sage.

Denzin, N. K., & Lincoln, Y. S. (2018). *The SAGE handbook of qualitative research* (5th ed.). Sage.

Dwyer, S. C., & Buckle, J. L. (2009). The space between: On being an insider-outsider in qualitative research. *International Journal of Qualitative Methods, 8*(1), 54–63. https://doi.org/10.1177/160940690900800105

Edvardsson, B., & Roos, I. (2001). Critical incident techniques: Towards a framework for analyzing the criticality of critical incidents. *International Journal of Service Industry Management, 12*(3–4), 251–268. https://doi.org/10.1108/EUM0000000005520

Edvardsson, B., & Strandvik, T. (2000). Is a critical incident critical for a customer relationship? *Managing Service Quality, 10*(2), 82–91. https://doi.org/10.1108/09604520010318272

Ellinger, A. D., & Bostrom, R. P. (2002). An examination of managers' beliefs about their roles as facilitators of learning. *Management Learning, 33*(2), 147–179. https://doi.org/10.1177/1350507602332001

Esposito, J., & Evans-Winters, V. (2022). *Introduction to intersectional qualitative research.* Sage.

Flanagan, J. C. (1947). *The aviation psychology program in the Army Air Forces.* AAF Aviation Psychology Program.

Flanagan, J. C. (1954). The critical incident technique. *Psychological Bulletin, 51*(4), 327–358. https://doi.org/10.1037/h0061470

Forsythe, A., & Lander, D. (2003). A reflexive inquiry of two non-smokers: A trans-generational tale of social gospel and social norms marketing. *Reflective Practice, 4*(2), 139–161. https://doi.org/10.1080/14623940308266

Fuglsang, L. (2017). The critical incident technique and everyday innovation. In F. Sorensen, & F. Lapenta (Eds.), *Research methods in service innovation* (pp. 40–59). Edward Elgar. https://doi.org/10.4337/9781785364860.00009

Gremler, D. D. (2004). The critical incident technique in service research. *Journal of Service Research, 7*(1), 65–89. https://doi.org/10.1177/1094670504266138

Grimes, D. (2001). Putting our own house in order: Whiteness, change and organization studies. *Journal of Organizational Change Management, 14*(2), 132–149. https://doi.org/10.1108/09534810110388054

Gubrium, J. F., Holstein, J. A., Marvasti, A., & McKinney, K. D. (2012). *The SAGE handbook of interview research: The complexity of the craft* (2nd ed.). Sage. https://doi.org/10.4135/9781452218403

Hensing, G. K. E., Sverker, A. M., & Leijon, G. S. (2007). Experienced dilemmas of everyday life in chronic neuropathic pain patients—Results from a critical incident study. *Scandinavian Journal of Caring Sciences, 21*(2), 147–154. https://doi.org/10.1111/j.1471-6712.2007.00450.x

Hoffman, K. D., & Chung, B. G. (1999). Hospitality recovery strategies: Customer preference versus firm use. *Journal of Hospitality & Tourism Research, 23*(1), 71–84. https://doi.org/10.1177/109634809902300106

Holloway, E. L., & Schwartz, H. L. (2014). Critical incident technique: Exploring meaningful interactions between students and professors. In *SAGE research methods cases* (Pt. 1). Sage. https://doi.org/10.4135/978144627305014533929

Holmes, A. G. D. (2020). Researcher positionality: A consideration of its influence and place in qualitative research—A new researcher guide. *Shanlax International Journal of Education, 8*(4), 1–10. https://doi.org/10.34293/education.v8i4.3232

Humble, J. (2023). *3 types of UX diagrams for visualizing qualitative data*. The Fountain Institute. https://www.thefountaininstitute.com/blog/3-types-of-ux-diagrams-for-visualizing-qualitative-data

Jacobson, D., & Mustafa, N. (2019). Social identity map: A reflexivity tool for practicing explicit positionality in critical qualitative research. *International Journal of Qualitative Methods, 18*. https://doi.org/10.1177/1609406919870075

Josselson, R. (2013). *Interviewing for qualitative inquiry: A relational approach*. Guilford Publications.

Kamal, F. M., Baharin, H., Adnan, W., Adilah, W., & Noor, N. (2021). Modified critical incident (MCIT): A means to uncover experience of mobile social messaging system using informant-specific cues. *Turkish Journal of Computer and Mathematics Education, 12*(3), 1899–1908.

Keatinge, D. (2002). Versatility and flexibility: Attributes of the critical incident technique in nursing research. *Nursing & Health Sciences, 4*(1–2), 33–39. https://doi.org/10.1046/j.1442-2018.2002.00099.x

Kellogg, A. H., & Liddell, D. L. (2012). "Not half but double": Exploring critical incidents in the racial identity of multiracial college students. *Journal of College Student Development, 53*(4), 524–541. https://doi.org/10.1353/csd.2012.0054

Kemppainen, J. K., O'Brien, L., & Corpuz, B. (1998). The behaviors of AIDS patients toward their nurses. *International Journal of Nursing Studies, 35*(6), 330–338. https://doi.org/10.1016/s0020-7489(98)00047-9

Kerstetter, K. (2012). Insider, outsider, or somewhere between: The impact of researchers' identities on the community-based research process. *Journal of Rural Social Sciences, 27*(2), 99–117. https://search.proquest.com/docview/1287032003

Lampley, K. P. (2023). *Experiencing workplace inclusion: Critical incidents that create a sense of inclusion for professional staff in higher education* [Doctoral dissertation, Antioch University]. OhioLINK ETD Center. https://rave.ohiolink.edu/etdc/view?acc_num=antioch1679595991625716

Levitt, H. M., Bamberg, M., Creswell, J. W., Frost, D. M., Josselson, R., & Suárez-Orozco, C. (2018). Journal article reporting standards for qualitative primary, qualitative meta-analytic, and mixed methods research in psychology: The APA Publications and Communications Board Task Force report. *American Psychologist, 73*(1), 26–46. https://doi.org/10.1037/amp0000151

Lincoln, Y. S., & Guba, E. G. (1985). *Naturalistic inquiry.* Sage.

Lincoln, Y. S., & Guba, E. G. (2013). *The constructivist credo.* Left Coast Press.

Lucas, L., Katiri, R., & Kitterick, P. T. (2018). The psychological and social consequences of single-sided deafness in adulthood. *International Journal of Audiology, 57*(1), 21–30. https://doi.org/10.1080/14992027.2017.1398420

Marshall, J. L. (2023). *Ain't I an anthropologist: Zora Neale Hurston beyond the literary icon.* University of Illinois Press.

Mathew, D., Nishikawara, R., Ferguson, A. O., & Borgen, W. A. (2023). Cultural infusions and shifting sands: What helps and hinders career decision-making of Indigenous young people. *Canadian Journal of Career Development, 22*(1), 6–18. https://doi.org/10.53379/cjcd.2023.345

McDaniel, M. M., Borgen, W. A., Buchanan, M. J., Butterfield, L. D., & Amundson, N. E. (2020). The philosophical underpinnings of the enhanced critical incident technique. *Canadian Journal of Counselling and Psychotherapy, 54*(4), 738–755. https://doi.org/10.47634/cjcp.v54i4.68139

McDaniel, S. H., Morse, D. S., Reis, S., Edwardsen, E. A., Gurnsey, M. G., Taupin, A., Griggs, J. J., & Shields, C. G. (2013). Physicians criticizing physicians to patients. *Journal of General Internal Medicine, 28*(11), 1405–1409. https://doi.org/10.1007/s11606-013-2499-9

Miles, M. B., & Huberman, A. M. (1994). *Qualitative data analysis* (2nd ed.). Sage.

Miles, M. B., Huberman, A. M., & Saldana, J. (2014). *Qualitative data analysis: A methods sourcebook* (4th ed.). Sage.

Milner, H. R., IV. (2007). Race, culture, and researcher positionality: Working through dangers seen, unseen, and unforeseen. *Educational Researcher, 36*(7), 388–400. https://doi.org/10.3102/0013189X07309471

Milner, J., Ostemeier, E., & Franke, R. (2013). Critical incidents in cross-cultural coaching: The view from German coaches. *International Journal of Evidence Based Coaching and Mentoring, 11*(2), 19–32. https://doaj.org/article/78ce99eefd194281a7f2cde67a1305ba

Morrow, S. L. (2005). Quality and trustworthiness in qualitative research in counseling psychology. *Journal of Counseling Psychology, 52*(2), 250–260. https://doi.org/10.1037/0022-0167.52.2.250

Morse, J. (2018). Reframing rigor in qualitative inquiry. In N. K. Denzin & Y. S. Lincoln (Eds.), *The SAGE handbook of qualitative research* (pp. 796–816). Sage.

Morse, J. M. (2015). Critical analysis of strategies for determining rigor in qualitative inquiry. *Qualitative Health Research, 25*(9), 1212–1222. https://doi.org/10.1177/1049732315588501

Norman, I. J., Redfern, S. J., Tomalin, D. A., & Oliver, S. (1992). Developing Flanagan's critical incident technique to elicit indicators of high and low quality nursing care from patients and their nurses. *Journal of Advanced Nursing, 17*(5), 590–600. https://doi.org/10.1111/j.1365-2648.1992.tb02837.x

Paxton, E. (2021). *Exploring the use of courageous followership in conversations with nurses and their colleagues* [Doctoral dissertation, Antioch University]. OhioLINK ETD Center. https://etd.ohiolink.edu/acprod/odb_etd/etd/r/1501/10?clear=10&p10_accession_num=antioch1634142953215113

Persson, M., & Mårtensson, J. (2006). Situations influencing habits in diet and exercise among nurses working night shift. *Journal of Nursing Management, 14*(5), 414–423. https://doi.org/10.1111/j.1365-2934.2006.00601.x

Petrucci, A. S., & Palombo, D. J. (2021). A matter of time: How does emotion influence temporal aspects of remembering? *Cognition and Emotion, 35*(8), 1499–1515. https://doi.org/10.1080/02699931.2021.1976733

Philpot, R., Smith, W., Gerdin, G., Larsson, L., Schenker, K., Linnér, S., Moen, K. M., & Westlie, K. (2021). Exploring social justice pedagogies in health and physical education through critical incident technique methodology. *European Physical Education Review, 27*(1), 57–75. https://doi.org/10.1177/1356336X20921541

Piccinelli, E., Martinho, S., & Vauclair, C. M. (2020). Expressions of microaggressions against women in the healthcare context: A critical incident approach. *PSIQUE, 1*, 44–64. https://doi.org/10.26619/2183-4806.XVI.1.3

Pociunaite, J., Zimprich, D., & Wolf, T. (2022). Centrality of positive and negative autobiographical memories across adult life span. *Applied Cognitive Psychology, 36*(3), 623–635. https://doi.org/10.1002/acp.3949

Roos, I. (1999). Switching processes in customer relationships. *Journal of Service Research, 2*(1), 68–85. https://doi.org/10.1177/109467059921006

Roos, I. (2002). Methods of investigating critical incidents. *Journal of Service Research, 4*(3), 193–204. https://doi.org/10.1177/1094670502004003003

Roulston, K. (2022). *Interviewing: A guide to theory and practice* (1st ed.). Sage.

Rubin, H. J., & Rubin, I. S. (2012). *Qualitative interviewing: The art of hearing data* (3rd ed.). Sage.

Saldana, J. (2013). *The coding manual for qualitative researchers* (2nd ed.). Sage.

Scagnoli, N. I., & Verdinelli, S. (2017). Editors' perspective on the use of visual displays in qualitative studies. *The Qualitative Report, 22*(7), 1945–1963. https://doi.org/10.46743/2160-3715/2017.2202

Schatzman, L. (1991). Dimensional analysis: Notes on an alternative approach to the grounding of theory in qualitative research. In A. Strauss & D. Maines (Eds.), *Social organization and social process: Essays in honor of Anselm Strauss* (pp. 303–314). de Gruyter.

Schluter, J., Seaton, P., & Chaboyer, W. (2008). Critical incident technique: A user's guide for nurse researchers. *Journal of Advanced Nursing, 61*(1), 107–114. https://doi.org/10.1111/j.1365-2648.2007.04490.x

Schwartz, H. L., & Holloway, E. L. (2014). "I became a part of the learning process": Mentoring episodes and individualized attention in graduate education. *The Mentoring and Tutoring Journal, 21*(1), 38–55. https://doi.org/10.1080/13611267.2014.882604

Sharoff, L. (2008). Critique of the critical incident technique. *Journal of Research in Nursing, 13*(4), 301–309. https://doi.org/10.1177/1744987107081248

Smith, J. A., Flowers, P., & Larkin, M. (2022). *Interpretative phenomenological analysis: Theory, method, and research* (2nd ed.). Sage.

Springer, K. L., & Bedi, R. P. (2021). Why do men drop out of counseling/psychotherapy? An enhanced critical incident technique analysis of male clients' experiences. *Psychology of Men & Masculinity, 22*(4), 776–786. https://doi.org/10.1037/men0000350

Stauss, B., & Weinlich, B. (1997). Process-oriented measurement of service quality Applying the sequential incident technique. *European Journal of Marketing, 31*(1), 33–55. https://doi.org/10.1108/03090569710157025

Stephenson, W. (2015). *Midnight running: How international human resource managers make meaning of expatriate adjustment* [Doctoral dissertation, University of Georgia]. https://getd.libs.uga.edu/pdfs/stephenson_wayne_t_201505_phd.pdf

Stinson, R. F. (2010). *Critical incidents that lead to homelessness: Recommendations for counselors* [Doctoral dissertation, University of Iowa]. Dissertations & Theses Europe Full Text: Social Sciences. https://www.riss.kr/pdu/ddodLink.do?id=T12691897

Tervalon, M., & Murray-García, J. (1998). Cultural humility versus cultural competence: A critical distinction in defining physician training outcomes in multicultural education. *Journal of Health Care for the Poor and Underserved, 9*(2), 117–125. https://doi.org/10.1353/hpu.2010.0233

Timmermans, S., & Tavory, I. (2012). Theory construction in qualitative research. *Sociological Theory, 30*(3), 167–186. https://doi.org/10.1177/0735275112457914

Verdinelli, S., & Scagnoli, N. I. (2013). Data display in qualitative research. *International Journal of Qualitative Methods, 12*(1), 359–381. https://doi.org/10.1177/160940691301200117

Viergever, R. F. (2019). The critical incident technique: Method or methodology? *Qualitative Health Research, 29*(7), 1065–1079. https://doi.org/10.1177/1049732318813112

Viscione, P. J. (2022). *Exploring the career advancement experience of Black women on their journey to executive levels in large American corporations* [Doctoral dissertation, Antioch University]. OhioLINK ETD Center. https://rave.ohiolink.edu/etdc/view?acc_num=antioch1667241414097326

Warrens, M. J. (2015). Five ways to look at Cohen's kappa. *Journal of Psychology & Psychotherapy, 5*(4), 197. https://doi.org/10.4172/2161-0487.1000197

Watkins, K. E., Ellinger, A. D., Suh, B., Brenes-Dawsey, J. C., & Oliver, L. C. (2022). Further evolving the critical incident technique (CIT) by applying different contemporary approaches for analyzing qualitative data in CIT studies. *European Journal of Training and Development, 46*(7/8), 709–726. https://doi.org/10.1108/EJTD-07-2021-0107

Willis, R. (2019). The use of composite narratives to present interview findings. *Qualitative Research, 19*(4), 471–480. https://doi.org/10.1177/1468794118787711

Woolgar, S. (2019). *Resolving occupational burnout: Exploring factors in personal recovery through an enhanced critical incident technique* [Master's thesis, University of British Columbia]. https://hdl.handle.net/2429/69551

Woolsey, L. K. (1986). The critical incident technique: An innovative qualitative method of research. *Canadian Journal of Counselling, 20*(4), 242–254.

Yonas, M. A., Aronson, R., Schaal, J., Eng, E., Hardy, C., & Jones, N. (2013). Critical incident technique: An innovative participatory approach to examine and document racial disparities in breast cancer healthcare services. *Health Education Research, 28*(5), 748–759. https://doi.org/10.1093/her/cyt082

Index

About the Authors

Harriet L. Schwartz, PhD, is a professor of relational practice and higher education at Antioch University's PhD in Leadership and Change program. Her scholarly interests include teaching as relational practice, emotion and teaching, and qualitative research methods, particularly critical incident technique and grounded theory. Harriet is the author of *Connected Teaching: Relationship, Power, and Mattering in Higher Education* (Stylus, 2019) and is a leader in applying relational cultural theory in education. She serves as lead scholar for education as relational practice and on the leadership team for the International Center for Growth in Connection. Along with numerous journal articles, Harriet has published two *New Directions for Teaching and Learning* sourcebooks, serving as coeditor of *Teaching and Emotion* and editor of *Interpersonal Boundaries in Teaching and Learning*. Harriet worked in student affairs for many years before transitioning to a faculty career. Along with teaching in leadership programs on the master's and doctoral levels, she has also taught in counseling, student affairs, and education graduate programs.

Elizabeth L. Holloway, PhD, professor emerita of Antioch University, has over 35 years of experience as a research scientist, practitioner, and consultant in clinical supervision, relational practice, and respectful workplaces. She has held professorships at the University of California, University of Utah, University of Oregon, University of Wisconsin, and Antioch University. During her academic career, Elizabeth has achieved distinction for her research and practice, including a Fellow of the American Psychological Association, a Diplomate of the American Board of Professional Psychology, and a recipient of the American Educational Research Association Research Award for Counseling. Her methodological expertise includes discourse analysis, grounded theory, narrative inquiry, critical incident technique, and case study design. She has authored or coauthored eight books. A recent update of her original supervision model, *Supervision Essentials for a Systems Approach to Supervision*, was published in 2016 (Chinese version in press). Her most recent work with coauthor Harriet Schwartz introduces a constructivist approach to critical incident technique methodology. Elizabeth teaches workshops on her model of clinical supervision and building respectful workplaces worldwide.